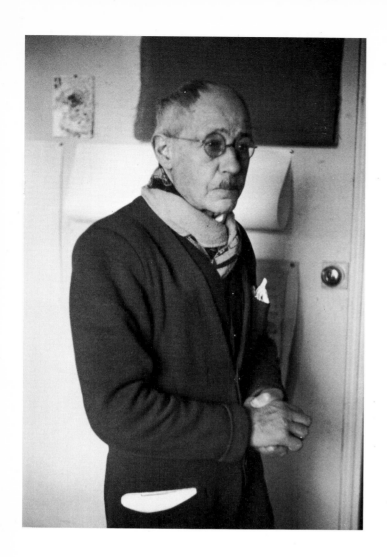

BONNARD

AND HIS ENVIRONMENT

Pierre Bonnard, 1944. © Henri Cartier-Bresson, Magnum

THE MUSEUM OF MODERN ART, NEW YORK, IN COLLABORATION WITH

BONNARD

AND HIS ENVIRONMENT

TEXTS BY JAMES THRALL SOBY, JAMES ELLIOTT, AND MONROE WHEELER

THE LOS ANGELES COUNTY MUSEUM OF ART AND THE ART INSTITUTE OF CHICAGO

DISTRIBUTED BY DOUBLEDAY & COMPANY, INC., GARDEN CITY, NEW YORK

CONTENTS

7   PREFACE AND ACKNOWLEDGMENTS

9   INTRODUCTION

14   BRIEF CHRONOLOGY

16   BIOGRAPHICAL COMMENT

22   BONNARD AND HIS ENVIRONMENT

63   COLOR PLATES

107   LENDERS TO THE EXHIBITION

107   CATALOGUE OF THE EXHIBITION

111   SELECTED BIBLIOGRAPHY

116   WORKS ILLUSTRATED BY BONNARD

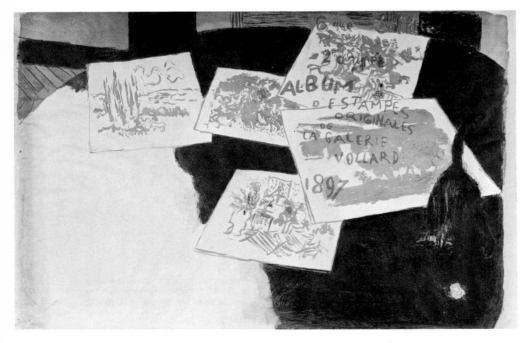

Cover for *L'Album d'estampes originales*, 1897. Color lithograph, 22 ¼ x 33 ½".
The Museum of Modern Art, New York. Purchase

PREFACE AND ACKNOWLEDGMENTS

THIS PUBLICATION RECORDS a joint effort of three museums to present a new survey of one of the greatest painters of our century in the three largest cities of the United States.

Bonnard's first one-man show outside France took place in New York when de Hauke & Co. showed forty of his paintings in 1928, two years after he had come to America to serve on the Carnegie International Jury in Pittsburgh, from which exhibition Mr. Duncan Phillips acquired the first of the thirty Bonnards he and his gallery in Washington now possess. Bonnard was first shown at The Museum of Modern Art two months after it opened when seven of his paintings were included in Alfred H. Barr, Jr.'s exhibition, "Painting in Paris," in January, 1930. The Art Institute of Chicago exhibited his work, with Vuillard's, in 1938. Los Angeles will see a major Bonnard exhibition for the first time when the present showing inaugurates the new buildings of the Los Angeles County Museum of Art.

It is the second Bonnard retrospective to be held at The Museum of Modern Art; the first one, in 1948, the year following the artist's death, was co-sponsored by The Cleveland Museum of Art and was directed by John Rewald who wrote for it the first comprehensive study of Bonnard in English. As this volume is still available, we have not attempted to provide a substitute for Mr. Rewald's thorough summing up of the artist's career.

On behalf of the Trustees of the three co-sponsoring museums, we wish to record our thanks to the museums and individuals (listed on page 107) who have graciously consented to part with their pictures for the long period required for a triple exhibition. We are indebted to the French Government for its official sponsorship of the exhibition through the Association Française d'Action Artistique. The artist's nephew, Mr. Charles Terrasse, Curator of the Museum of Fontainebleau, and Mr. Jean Cassou,

Chief Curator of the National Museum of Modern Art in Paris, gave us inspiring encouragement and provided information not previously available. Many of Bonnard's admirers have contributed to our research, and we are particularly grateful to the following persons who have either worked with us directly upon the exhibition or provided valuable information and photographs:

Mr. Ronald Alley, Mr. Alfred H. Barr, Jr., Miss Gisèle Belleud, Mr. and Mrs. Georges Bernier, Mr. Georges Besson, Miss Francoise Boas, Mr. Richard F. Brown, Mr. Louis Carré, Mr. Henri Cartier-Bresson, Miss Riva Castleman, Mr. Gerald Corcoran, Mr. Larry Curry, Mr. Henry Dauberville, Mr. Jean Dauberville, Mr. François Dault, Mr. Bernard Dorival, Miss Helen M. Franc, Mr. Gilbert Gruet, Mrs. Charles Jaggli-Hahnloser, Professor Dr. Hans R. Hahnloser, Miss Nadia Hermos, Mr. Philippe Huisman, Mr. Phillip James, Mr. Harold Joachim, Mrs. Suzanne Kahn, Miss Frances Keech, Mr. Emil Langui, Miss Alicia Legg, Mr. William S. Lieberman, Mr. Frank Lloyd, Mr. John Maxon, Mr. Edouard Morot-Sir, Mr. Willy Peplow, Miss Frances Pernas, Miss Carolyn Pettit, Mr. John Rewald, Mr. Helmut Ripperger, Dr. Henry R. Roland, Mr. Alexandre Rosenberg, Sir John Rothenstein, Mr. Franco Russoli, Mr. Sam Salz, Mr. Peter Selz, Mr. William C. Seitz, Mr. James Thrall Soby, Miss Nicole Villa, Mr. Leslie Waddington, Dr. R. Wehrli, Mr. Glenway Wescott, Mr. Daniel Wildenstein, Mr. Sigurd Willoch, Mr. A. Campbell Wylly, Mr. Charles Zadok.

Co-directors of the Exhibition:

> JAMES ELLIOTT, *Chief Curator, Los Angeles County Museum of Art*
>
> MONROE WHEELER, *Director of Exhibitions and Publications, The Museum of Modern Art, New York*

Entrance to *Le Bosquet*, Bonnard's home at Le Cannet, 1944. © Henri Cartier-Bresson, Magnum

INTRODUCTION

IT IS A PARADOX of Pierre Bonnard's long and most distinguished career that in the United States, where the French impressionists found a number of early and fervent champions, their spiritual heir, Bonnard, has only lately come to great fame. His professional career began in the early 1890s, and yet for almost fifty years there was no public or private collection here where his works could be seen in number except in the Phillips Collection in Washington, D. C. Perhaps his art was too French for our taste, though this is hard to believe considering the fact that from the date of the Armory Show (1913) to the outbreak of World War II the School of Paris dominated the American art scene. Possibly our taste for visual revolution, once aroused, found Bonnard belated in aim. At any rate his following and patronage remained predominantly European until after the war. He was revered in Paris by colleagues we had long since taken to our hearts, yet we seemed unwilling to believe in their faith. As a case in point, in 1947 *Cahiers d'Art* in Paris published an article on Bonnard entitled "Pierre Bonnard—est-il un grand peintre?" The article concluded: "How to explain the reputation of Bonnard's work? . . . It is evident that this reverence is shared only by people who know nothing about the grave difficulties of art and cling above all to what is facile and agreeable." A stinging rebuttal was sent at once to the magazine by no less a world figure than Henri Matisse. Pierre Matisse tells me that he had seldom seen his father so angry.

Bonnard's art was of course the opposite of facile. It was painstaking and meditative to an extraordinary degree. One does not easily forget the story of Bonnard persuading his friend Vuillard to distract the guards in the Luxembourg Museum while he surreptitiously retouched one of his paintings which had been in the museum's collection for many years.

Bonnard's conscience was profound, his longing for perfection unrelenting. His instinctive modesty forced him to dislike personal flamboyance. He reserved daring—and it was often an extreme daring —for what he painted or drew. We have only begun to understand in this country what intimates like Vuillard and Matisse knew all along; namely, that a convinced flouting of conventions of color and form was quite as important a part of Bonnard's achievement as his unmistakable intimacy and charm. Once he looked intently at a picture by a predecessor and asked the owner of the gallery, "What do you want with a poor painting of mine, when you have in that canvas all that painting can be?" The picture in question was not by Claude Monet, to whose art of the later 1880s Bonnard's own seems most closely related. It was by Paul Cézanne. If Cézanne's influence on his younger countryman is impossible to determine precisely, the fact remains that the two men shared a mistrust of regimented values which some painters proclaim by abrupt defiance, others by quiet desertion from the ranks.

Girls. (c.1893). Pen and ink, 10 x 14″.
Frank Perls Gallery, Beverly Hills, California

Circus Horse. (1946). Oil, 37 x 46½".
Private collection, Paris

When pondering the bolder aspects of Bonnard's art, I usually think first of his *Circus Horse*, completed the year before he died. In youth he had often painted horses, but for the most part they were ancient hacks drawing carriages along Paris' quieter streets. The muscular tensions of race-track thoroughbreds left him indifferent, whereas they had fascinated Degas and Lautrec. The truth is that Bonnard's basic domesticity of vision extended to almost all aspects of life in his time. And yet his *Circus Horse* is not easily dislodged from memory. It is opposite in spirit to the ghostly, malignant stallion which looms through the window in Fuseli's famous *Nightmare* of 1782. Nevertheless, its effect is scarcely less obsessive, the buffoonery of the horse's absurdly elongated head unforgettable. Bonnard's image proves again that great humor can strike at our consciousness nearly as hard as terror.

It would be an untenable exaggeration to refer to Bonnard as an *animalier* in the sense that the word was understood by earlier generations of artists. The fact remains that animals appear in his pictures repeatedly. His favorite was the small, affectionate dachshund which sidles into many of his composi-

tions and whose silhouette often acts as a complement to family relaxation. Bonnard was equally fond of cats. He liked them as beguiling pets and not for their capacity to become stand-ins for their jungle cousins, as did Delacroix. Bonnard was too late in time to share the Romantics' ardor for imperious steeds and for wild beasts caged in Paris zoos or running free in the African veldt. His interest was in animals to be held in the lap.

As already noted, Bonnard began to paint professionally in the early 1890s, as did his lifelong friend, Vuillard. It always comes as something of a shock to remember that Toulouse-Lautrec was so nearly the contemporary of these two artists; he was only three years older than Bonnard; he was Vuillard's elder by four. I assume our confusion arises from the fact that Lautrec has always been closely identified with *fin-de-siècle* esthetics, whereas his slightly junior colleagues have not. Lautrec outlived his astonishingly self-contained decade by a mere year.

Vuillard and Bonnard went on and on, the former with dwindling authority for the most part, the latter with uninterrupted ascendancy to the end of his long life. Like most good artists Bonnard had his vintage years. He almost never had one during which his creative yield was thin or bitter.

Bonnard and Vuillard were devoted friends throughout their long careers. Indeed there was a durability of affection and respect among leaders of their generation which exploded into recrimination with their successors in the School of Paris. In youth the two friends were allied in the movement called "the Nabis"—the Hebrew word for prophets. As happens sporadically in art history, far less talented painters—Paul Sérusier and Maurice Denis —were the movement's most effective polemicists.

The Nabis met often, seeking the warmth of mutual aim and faith. In most accounts of their mildly insurrectionary gatherings Vuillard is described as restrained and rather morose, Bonnard as incurably gay. Members of the group had nicknames and Bonnard was known as "the very Japanese Nabi" because of his devotion to Oriental calligraphy in general and Japanese prints in particular. Later on, I think, the nickname took on a new and perhaps more profound meaning. For Bonnard was to emerge as a pearl diver among artists of his generation. In numerous works of his later career he discovered a nacreous quality in objects that the tides of familiarity had clouded or covered with habit's blind sand.

In youth Vuillard may well have been the more original of the two friends. He was apparently indifferent to or at least not deeply moved by the tonal subtleties of plane which were Cézanne's obsession. Instead, perhaps with Gauguin's more recent example in mind, he hung sheets of restrained and bland color one behind another and somehow kept them separate in air and space. I suppose his was essentially an intaglio process; I cannot think of any artist since who has used his system of pleated perspective, one stiff fold succeeding another as in an opened accordion, with his deftness and control. Vuillard's difficulty was that in later life he became cautious and precise to such a degree that one of his many celebrated portrait subjects asked her maid to remove some medicine from her bedside table "because M. Vuillard paints everything he sees."

Bonnard, on the contrary, grew more and more absorbed in fugitive and delicate forms of observation. These forms were once well described by Clive Bell, to my mind an underrated critic because of today's sometimes obtuse preference for architectonic, over-poetic, or sensual values. Bell wrote: "There is something Chinese about him [Bonnard]; and he is one of those rare Europeans who have dealt in 'imposed' rather than 'built-up' design. Bonnard's pictures as a rule grow not as trees; they float as water lilies. European pictures, as a rule, spring upwards, masonry-wise, from their foundation; the design of a picture by Bonnard, like that of many Chinese pictures and Persian textiles, seems to have been laid on the canvas as one might lay cautiously on dry grass some infinitely precious figured gauze."

After his youth as the friend in Paris of artists, writers, magazine editors, and impresarios of the stage, Bonnard spent most of his life in country houses throughout France. He tended to restrict his range of subject matter to daily scenes relating to life in the towns and resorts of his native land. He also restricted himself still further in the themes he chose. Whereas Vuillard as a bachelor had a lively interest in the salons of urbane houses where he was welcome as a distinguished guest, Bonnard preferred the rooms of family intimacy—the kitchen, the bedroom, the bath. In this preference he was the almost total opposite of Lautrec, who so disliked home life that he could hardly wait to bolt out the door and seek in hired warmth the affection his mother tried to give him and his monstrous father did his best to destroy.

Another recurrent element in Bonnard's iconography was related to his liking for uncomplicated domesticity. It was food. Not food as prepared by the great restaurants of France so much as food prepared at home by a skilled housewife or maid. He obviously loved the aromas of family kitchens. And in this connection there is a fact to be noted. Bonnard was apparently awed by the luminosity of the Dutch Little Masters, who were perpetually concerned with food and drink as subjects for their art. Yet whereas the seventeenth-century Hollanders liked to paint food on large tables, awaiting preparation, Bonnard was equally if not more interested in the feast itself. Though he often painted the separate ingredients of a fine luncheon or dinner, he seemed to be looking forward in imagination to the final repast. In 1910 or thereabouts, for example, he did a sumptuous picture called *La Bouillabaisse*. The components of the classic Mediterranean stew are assembled uncooked on a kitchen table, and a cat looks on voraciously. But the room is already pungent with the steam of the finished dish in its tureen. If the frail skin of onions and the shimmer of goblets are subjects that have fascinated artists for centuries, they have not often been given so acute an aura of physical anticipation as Bonnard was able to give. Few modern artists have so consistently transformed ordinary pleasures into ecstasy.

Bonnard was also much preoccupied with one of the most traditional of art's subjects—the female nude. His approach to the theme was for him exceptionally diverse in mood. He painted a number of reclining nudes which are as playfully innocent as half-awakened kittens; he painted a few which are stridently erotic. Like Degas before him he delighted in the awkwardly beautiful gestures of women drying themselves after a bath. And he sometimes showed nudes in more conventional poses, their audience consisting of their own reflection in a mirror. In his attitude toward the nude he was more student than voyeur. His nudes with few exceptions lack the sensual impact of those of Matisse; they delight more than arouse.

In a great number of Bonnard's paintings there is a curious and highly inventive use of what can only be called a hide-and-seek solution as to what is meant to be on view. Time after time in viewing his work one feels a sense of apparition, as when what one assumed to be "abstract" decorative elements turn into human figures or animals, sometimes only after prolonged observation. The process is not to be confused with the technique of double imagery, in which one or more forms are suddenly metamorphosed into others of different identity. Instead Bonnard plays an extremely subtle game of disguise in which figures or objects, once found, never disappear again but hold their own character completely. There are many interiors by Bonnard, for example, at which one must look repeatedly before being certain how many people are in the room. The light is uniformly clear; some of the figures are immediately visible, yet others are illusive phantoms, as if only at the last moment allowed to edge past a given composition's borders.

As a landscape painter Bonnard seems to me to have been most successful when he worked on a modest scale. His huge panoramic murals of fields or sea, however brilliant in certain passages, tend toward emptiness and over extension. It could be

The Loge. (1898). Frontispiece for Mellerio's *Lithographie originale en couleurs.* Color lithograph, 8 ¼ x 7 ⁷⁄₁₆″.
The Museum of Modern Art, New York.
Gift of Mrs. Edith G. Halpert

that Bonnard was aware of the fact and tried to enliven such pictures by mythological or allegorical allusions, perhaps following the example of the later Maurice Denis or of Vuillard's brother-in-law, Roussel. The remedy did not always work. Bonnard seems to me to have been more sure of himself as a landscapist when he could begin with a sense of enclosure, as when a garden is seen through an open door. If true, the fact seems curious in that Bonnard's capacity for concentration and limitation of vision was miraculous. In The Museum of Modern Art's admirable monograph on Bonnard by John Rewald there is reproduced a 1937 photograph of a room at Deauville in which the artist worked. Paintings which he was completing are tacked on the wall over wallpaper of a violently aggressive, flowered design. As Rewald suggests, it is astonishing that Bonnard was able to focus on his own compositions when seen against so insistent a background. But he was. One does not know what blinders against distraction he wore; one knows how well they worked.

As a final matter, it would be interesting to think how Bonnard would have fared if he had lived in an epoch when portraiture was a persistent rather than marginal concern of leading artists. His portraits are limited in number and the best of them are of friends. The finest of all, it seems to me, are those he did of himself. Especially toward the end of his life he painted a few self-portraits in which his shy intensity of personality comes through with memorable vivacity. Their mood varies between quizzical aloofness and solemn introspection. In either case they have exceptional tenacity as images.

Perhaps both moods were typical of Bonnard's inner character. It would seem so from accounts of him by close friends. His lack of pretense has become proverbial, his simplicity quite likely overemphasized. For those of us who have loved his pictures for a long time, he is one of the enduring masters of French art.

JAMES THRALL SOBY

Child with Lamp. (1896). Color lithograph, 13⅛ x 18⅛″.
The Museum of Modern Art,
New York. Gift of Mrs. Bliss Parkinson

BRIEF CHRONOLOGY

1867 Born October 3, in Fontenary-aux-Roses, near Paris. His father came from the Dauphiné and headed an office in the War Ministry; his mother came from Alsace.

1877- Receives classical education at lycées de Vanves, Louis-le-
1887 Grand, and Charlemagne, and in Paris enters law school. Begins sketching.

1888 Curtails law studies to work at Ecole des Beaux-Arts and Académie Julian, where he meets Vuillard, Roussel, Denis, Vallotton, Ranson, and Sérusier. The latter, inspired by Gauguin, organizes his friends into a group called the "Nabis" (prophets).

1889- First studio: rue Le Chapelais. Military service at Bour-
1890 goile, where he meets the composer Claude Terrasse, whom Bonnard's sister soon marries. Receives 100 francs for champagne poster. Meets Toulouse-Lautrec. Shares studio with Vuillard and Denis, 28 rue Pigalle.

1891- Exhibits paintings at *Salon des Indépendants* and, with Nabis,
1894 at Le Barc de Boutteville's Gallery. Is discovered by critics Gustave Geffroy and Roger Marx. 1893: Makes poster, drawings, and lithographs for *La Revue Blanche*. Meets dealer Ambroise Vollard. Studio, 65 rue de Douai.

1895 Vollard publishes lithographs, *Quelques aspects de la vie de Paris*. Designs stained-glass window for Louis Comfort Tiffany.

1896 First one-man show, at Durand-Ruel's (49 paintings, prints, posters).

1897 In group show at Vollard's. Draws illustrations for Peter Nanson's *Marie* for *La Revue Blanche*. Vollard issues album of his lithographs.

1898 First showing abroad, with van Gogh, Gauguin, and Vuillard, in Oslo, Stockholm, and Göteborg.

1899 Bernheim-Jeune et Cie., becomes his dealer, a lifelong relationship. Visits Roussel often in L'Etang-la-ville. Studios: rue Le Chapelais and rue Ballu.

1900 Vollard publishes Verlaine's *Parallèlment*, with 109 lithographs and 9 wood engravings by Bonnard. In group exhibition at Bernheim-Jeune's.

1902 Vollard publishes *Daphnis and Chloé*, with 160 lithographs by Bonnard.

1903 Studio: 65 rue de Douai.

1904 One-man show at Bernheim-Jeune's, first of a dozen held at the gallery between 1904 and 1933. Draws 67 illustrations for Jules Renard's *Histoires Naturelles*.

1905- André Gide praises his paintings at the *Salon d'Automne*.
1906 Begins spending summers at Villennes and Vernouillet in the Seine Valley and Cotteville in Normandy.

1907 Paris studio: 60 rue de Douai. Between 1907 and 1911 takes short trips to Belgium, Holland, England, Italy, Spain, and Tunisia.

1908 Sale of Natanson collection, including 19 paintings by Bonnard which bring an average of 810 francs each.

1910 4 decorative panels for Missia Godebska shown at *Salon d'Automne*. Studios: 60 rue de Douai, 21 quai Voltaire.

1911 One-man show, Durand-Ruel's (27 paintings; also 3 decorative panels, later shown at *Salon d'Automne*).

1912 Buys small house, *Ma Roulotte*, at Vernonnet, near Vernon. Until 1938 divides time between Seine Valley and the south (Grasse, St. Tropez, Le Cannet). Paris studio: 22 rue Tourlaque.

1913 Travels in Holland and, with Vuillard, in England.

1914- During First World War lives mostly in Saint-Germain-
1918 en-Laye.

1919 First book on Bonnard, by Léon Werth. Paris address: 56 rue Molitor, Auteuil.

1922 Represented at Venice Biennale.

1923 Wins third prize, Carnegie International Exhibition, Pittsburgh.

1924 Retrospective exhibition at Gallery Druet, Paris (68 works).

1925 Marries his lifelong companion Marthe de Méligny (Maria Boursin). Buys villa *Le Bosquet* at Le Cannet. Paris residence: 48 Blvd. des Batignolles.

1926 To U.S.A. as juror for Carnegie International Exhibition.

1928 First one-man show outside France, at de Hauke & Co., New York (40 paintings).

1930 First showing at The Museum of Modern Art, New York (7 paintings in exhibition "Painting in Paris"). Vollard publishes his *La Vie de Sainte Monique*, with 29 drawings (transferred on stone), 17 etchings, and 178 compositions (drawn on wood), by Bonnard.

1932 Bonnard-Vuillard exhibition at Kunsthaus, Zurich. One-man exhibition at Galerie Braun et Cie., Paris (40 portraits). 1932-38: Summers in Deauville and Trouville; winters in Le Cannet.

1934 One-man show at Wildenstein's, New York (44 paintings).

1936 Wins second prize at Carnegie International Exhibition.

1938 Bonnard-Vuillard exhibition at The Art Institute of Chicago.

1939 Retrospective exhibition at Svensk-Franska Gallery,

Stockholm (51 paintings). After outbreak of war, Bonnard stays in Le Cannet.

1940 Death of Vuillard.

1942 Death of Madame Bonnard, January 26.

1945 Short visit to Paris.

1946 Retrospective exhibition at Bernheim-Jeune's (34 works). Consents to large retrospective at The Museum of Modern Art, New York, to celebrate his eightieth birthday.

1947 Death of Bonnard, January 23, in Le Cannet. The artist's nephew, Charles Terrasse, arranges large memorial exhibitions at the Carlsberg Glyptothek, Copenhagen; Stedelijk Museum, Amsterdam (77 works), and the Orangerie in Paris (197 works). Exhibition at Svensk-Franska Gallery, Stockholm (53 works).

1949 Exhibition, Kunsthaus, Zurich (247 works).

1950 Exhibition, Bernheim-Jeune's (62 works).

1951 Exhibition, Kunsthalle, Berne (76 works).

1953 Exhibition, Museum Boymans, Rotterdam (129 works).

1954 Exhibition, Lyon Musée (106 works).

1955 Exhibitions: Kunsthalle, Basel (173 works); Palazzo Reale, Milan (103 works); Musée des Ponchettes, Nice (78 works); Maison de la Pensée Française, Paris (45 works); "Bonnard, Vuillard et les Nabis, 1888-1903," Musée National d'Art Moderne, Paris.

1956 Exhibitions: Kunstverein, Brunswick, Germany (96 works); Bernheim-Jeune's (58 works).

Swan, illustration for *Histoires Naturelles* (p. 65). (1904). Brush and ink, 12 1/8 x 7 1/2". Collection Mr. and Mrs. Seth Dennis, Westport, Connecticut

BIOGRAPHICAL COMMENT

THE LIFE OF PIERRE BONNARD was extraordinarily private, with little dramatic incident and no major changes of vocation or destiny from beginning to end. Just as his lifework of painting has an essential continuity and homogeneity, his biography is all of a piece, and does not lend itself interestingly to narrative form. He himself was of little assistance as to particular problems of Bonnard scholarship; he did not remember such things precisely and, as a rule, did not even date his pictures.

His father was a government official of some importance in the War Ministry. Presumably to please him, in his early twenties Bonnard studied law, but simultaneously also went to art school. When it came time for his oral law examinations, he failed. After that he worked as a clerk in a government office for several months.

Then he sold a work of art: a color lithograph designed as a champagne poster for a Reims wine-merchant, for which he received a hundred francs. "A glorious event," as he recalled it years later; it emboldened him to declare to his father that he was not going to be able to become a lawyer or a bureaucrat; he was an artist. Presumably his family gave him some financial support during his noviti-ate. He soon began to sell his paintings, and less than a decade later signed an advantageous contract with an important dealer. His way of life was never extravagant; he seems never to have been troubled about money.

At twenty-eight he became intimate with a young woman who called herself Marthe de Méligny, although her name in fact was Maria Boursin; and their relationship (without marriage ceremony until 1925) went on uninterruptedly until her death. According to Bonnard's nephew, Charles Terrasse, it is she who appears in his pictures, early and late, more than anyone else: a woman of beautiful bodily proportions and peculiar grace, "fleeting and free,

of which the great observer's eye would always catch a gesture, a movement, or an undulation in the light."

Thadée Natanson, one of the far-sighted early collectors of Bonnard's work, has described her even more graphically: "Close to him, in exiguous quarters, we saw fluttering that young woman, then still a child, with whom he spent his life. She already had, and kept always, her wild look of a bird, her movement on tiptoe, as though wingèd. . . ." She was somewhat neurotic, he suggests, "alarming everyone around her (and herself) about her health." Others who knew her have spoken of her self-absorption, verging on unfriendliness and isolation, and of the fanatic care she took of herself and her extreme cleanliness. And thus Bonnard painted her, at her ablutions, or as a haunting presence, sometimes almost unnoticeable in a corner or partly beyond the frame, peering into the picture.

The best description of Bonnard himself, in the prime of life, is also Natanson's: "This slim, active man seems tall, although he stoops a little and folds up on himself. . . . He strokes his short beard which curls loosely on his obstinate chin. . . . His near-sightedness is that of an observer, but it eliminates useless details. Behind his spectacles, unusually lively pupils glance at or fix upon successive objects, to make them his own."

He was physically strong, fond of bicyling and boating, and to the end of his life would always go for a walk before breakfast, as a devout man goes to mass. He was devout, in his own way, about landscape, ever-renascent light, and the spectrum in everything; these, indeed, were fundamentals of his lifework. To use an old formula of the philosophers, he put his faith in "the coherence of Nature and Art"; and, of course, in his experience and pictorial predilection, human nature was a part of the whole—indoors and outdoors constantly communicating.

Family Scene. 1893. Color lithograph, 12 ⅜ x 7 ⅛".
The Museum of Modern Art, New York. Purchase

Aside from his vocation of painting there were two sides to his life: the enthralled and responsible life-long marital relationship, and a physical restlessness which took him from place to place, sometimes abroad, but especially in France, with a true love of his native land in all its wonderfully differentiated parts. He always maintained a home base in Paris—nine addresses of studios and apartments are known to us—but as his life went on, he spent more and more of the year elsewhere, in the valley of the Seine, in Normandy, and in the Midi. During most of the war years, 1914-18, he more or less regularly spent the winters in the south of France, at Antibes, Cannes, Grasse, and St. Tropez and finally at Le Cannet, where in 1925 he bought the small Villa du Bosquet, on a hill overlooking Cannes. But he still moved about, summering at La Baule or Deauville or Arcachon; also frequenting various watering places at other seasons.

One reason for this mobility was Bonnard's enjoyment of motoring. In 1911 he acquired a ten horse-power Renault, and on his first excursion in it drove straight to Mont Saint-Michel. Thereafter he was a confirmed motorist. In 1912 when he bought a

house in Vernonnet called "Ma Roulotte," his first improvement of it was the installation of a modern bathroom for Madame Bonnard; then he added a garage for himself. He was a leisurely driver, often covering as little as thirty miles a day, stopping frequently, sketching here and there, spending the night where convenient.

While he did not always work when he traveled, his eye for landscape never ceased to explore and accumulate pictorial material. Harry Lachman, an American painter, once invited him to go on a painting expedition across the Italian border. He arrived with all his own equipment: paintbox, canvases, portable easel. Bonnard, to his surprise, appeared on the threshold with no such impedimenta. Lachman had assumed that he was going to paint, but with what? Bonnard brushed this question aside, saying, as he seated himself contentedly in the car, "Moi, j'observe."

Except for Vuillard whom he always loved and admired, his relations with fellow painters were mutually respectful, cordial in some cases, but not close. His champagne poster impressed Toulouse-Lautrec, who sought him out and recommended his

Portrait. (c. 1893). Lithograph, 11 ½ x
9 ¾″, projected print for *L'Escarmouche.*
The Museum of Modern Art, New
York. Gift of Abby Aldrich Rockefeller

early pictures to prospective purchasers. Pissarro on the other hand disliked his first exhibition, and in a letter to his son declared that Monet and Renoir shared his adverse opinion. They all came around to a better appreciation of his talent later. Renoir inscribed to him two small paintings, which he would show to visitors with pride and admiring comment.

One day late in his life, somewhat discontentedly examining a painting by Rouault, he remarked to Louis Carré, "Rouault wasn't as lucky as I. He didn't know Renoir, who used to say to me, 'You must beautify things, Bonnard, always beautify!'"

He has been called the last of the impressionists—and so described himself to Matisse—but of course never followed in their footsteps exactly. But like Renoir and like Matisse he was not afraid of its being said that he painted too happily and decoratively. "One is not always transported with joy by what one sees," he told Tériade, "but a painter must be able to discern some agreeable connection between one thing and another, and to find a place for it in his painting. We can abstract beauty out of everything."(bibl. 184)

Some of his pictures were completed in short order, a matter of hours or days after he started them; but as a rule he kept them in view a long while and improved them little by little. Terrasse tells us that, in his middle period, the greater part of his work was begun while traveling around, but finished in the studio. Often he made use of a single great length of canvas which he affixed to the wall wherever he happened to be, marking on it different-sized areas for various pictures. At the end of his sojourn he would roll it up, put it in his car, unroll it again when he got home, and later cut it up.

The longer he lived the more he concentrated on color; stronger and stronger combinations of juxtaposed or superimposed pigment. Sometimes, having mixed one of his burning hues, vermilion or magenta or violet blue or peacock blue, and applied it to the work in progress, he would wander around the house from canvas to canvas, finding little places where he could insert what he had left over. As he himself said, a given color is very different when you see it with other colors adjacent. André Girard tells us that when Rouault retouched his pictures to improve them he called it "Bonnard-ing."(bibl. 77)

In 1943 he told Angèle Lamotte that often, when a painter gets to painting, what his picture portrays is an embarrassment to him. "The point of departure for a work of art is an idea," and in the presence of his subject matter, there is always a danger of the artist's becoming involved in immediacies and incidentals. She then asked whether he never painted with his subject before him. "Oh, yes, but I leave it," he answered, "and come back to it later.

I never let myself become absorbed in the reality. . . . In fact there is always some conflict between the initial concept, which is the right one, the painter's own, and the varied and ever variable world. . . .'' (bibl. 184)

In every reality that seemed to him worth representing, he was struck by some aspect which perhaps no one else would have noticed. During the war he told André Suarès, ''I've discovered peaches. They're so intense and soft, and some of them resemble a setting sun; only it's a sunset that does not disappear, which is most convenient for a painter.'' (bibl. 77)

He never imagined a picture in the abstract, but, on the other hand, he wanted the texture and substance of every square inch of his painting as such to be strong and sumptuous, though at the expense of recognizability. Upon occasion, concentrating to excess, he slipped into awkwardnesses, misrepresentations. He liked to have under his eyes in the studio any such exaggerated pictures. He said to

André Girard, ''It is important to keep one's failures; they present problems that I find passionately interesting.'' (bibl. 77)

Though stubborn about such idiosyncracies, he would speak of them apologetically. Once he said to Emile Compard, a young painter of his acquaintance, ''If you only knew what trouble I have drawing things!'' and gave as an example the time someone had called his attention to the fact that, in a standing nude belonging to Félix Fénéon, he had given the figure two right feet. But he had not changed it. ''After all, somehow, it seems to me better like that. It makes an interesting shape.'' (bibl. 264) Upon another occasion he said, ''At times the faults in a picture are what give it life.'' (bibl. 184)

In some pictures he applied color until he achieved the dense effect of barbaric jewelry or oriental fabric. In others, even on a large scale, he kept to the thinness and rapidity of watercolor, often expressing a preference for a sketchier work. Compard

Boating. (c. 1897). Color lithograph, 10 9/16 x 18 1/2''. The Museum of Modern Art, New York. Gift of Abby Aldrich Rockefeller

proudly recalls the elder painter's wanting to acquire one of his pictures. "Would you like me to pay for it," Bonnard asked, "or shall we make an exchange?" Wisely, Compard preferred a Bonnard, no matter how slight, to his own current market price, and finally had to choose between a small basket of green gages or a small nude. He decided on the nude. "Bravo!" cried Bonnard. "In the still life I have worked over the paint, whereas the nude is only a sketch. But I like a canvas not to look wearied by the brush." (bibl. 264)

In the chosen picture, he went on to say, he had expressed what he had in mind, then stopped. "I couldn't have given it another touch, which is rare for me," he added laughingly. "I always carry in my pocket a little box with some colors ready in it.

When I come across one of my canvases that displeases me, out comes my little box, and I fix it." In his old age he confessed to Girard that, in his opinion, his pictures still lacked "form, accent, and a skeleton. . . . I am just beginning to understand what it is to paint. A painter should have two lives, one in which to learn, and one in which to practice his art." (bibl. 77)

The German occupation in the late spring of 1940 scattered most of Bonnard's Paris friends; Vuillard died in June; and thereafter Bonnard preferred to stay in the south of France the year round. Madame Bonnard died on January 6, 1942. At the end of the war he returned to the metropolis for a while, but it no longer suited him. He went back to Le Cannet, and there the end came on January 23, 1947.

Laundry Girl. (1896). Charcoal, 12 ¼ x 7 ¾".
Private collection, Paris

The Laundry Girl. 1896. Color lithograph, 11 ⅜ x 7 ⅞".
The Museum of Modern Art, New York.
Gift of Victor S. Riesenfeld

The close of Bonnard's life was marked by a singular incident having to do with the inheritance of his pictures. When at last he married Marthe de Méligny, on August 13, 1925, it was according to a provision of French law called "communauté des biens"— joint ownership. She had always given him to understand that she had no living relatives; it was only when he married her that he learned her real name. She never made a will. After her death he found to his dismay and distress that, as a consequence of her intestacy, all his work would have to be listed and appraised and placed under seal.

Resenting the formalities of law involved—under the misleading advice of a lawyer, and confident that he was not acting to anyone's disadvantage—he drew up a will in her behalf, bequeathing to himself what surely belonged to him morally. He signed the will with her name, but did not attempt to disguise his own handwriting, and ingenuously even dated it six months after her death. Nevertheless, it was accepted by the local authorities, and thus he was able to conclude his life serenely, with no further uneasiness about the paintings in his possession.

As it happened, he possessed a great many. Both he and Vuillard had enjoyed a certain success prior to the First World War and had saved money, which dwindled to nothing in the inflation of the twenties. Whereupon they decided that, in lieu of other investments, they would simply keep a part of their artistic production.

The irregularity of Bonnard's situation inevitably came to light after his death, when it was discovered that Madame Bonnard had four nieces. At first it seemed possible that the entire estate might go to these ladies, because of the falsification of the will. A difficult sequence of litigations ensued, concluded by a compromise sixteen years later, when the pictures were divided between Bonnard's own family and his wife's.

MONROE WHEELER

Young Girl with Black Stockings. (1893). Lithograph, 11 7/16 x 5 1/16", published in *L'Escarmouche*, January 14, 1894. The Museum of Modern Art, New York. Gift of Abby Aldrich Rockefeller

BONNARD AND HIS ENVIRONMENT

PIERRE BONNARD DIED IN 1947, and since that time the recognition of his greatness has spread in widening circles. Along with this recognition has come the realization that his vision far transcended the charm and intimacy for which it received early praise. In seemingly gentle investigations of a modest environment, Bonnard produced works of art that are both monumental and lyrical, works that expand the insight as well as the formal devices of the impressionists in a profound and original way. His evolution offers an extended and natural transition from impressionism to abstraction that omits, or appears to omit, everything in between.

Bonnard never repudiated or openly defied the conventional French milieu in which he grew up. Living on his own terms behind a screen of charm and nonchalance, following his own path with quiet tenacity, he celebrated both in his life and in his art the amusements and tranquil pleasures of French middleclass life. It was a life in which gratification of the senses was easily accepted. The hedonism that pervades the world of his art, however, is a moderate hedonism, which he presents (especially in interior scenes) with a questioning undertone. Although in his early work he chides his milieu for its foibles with a sly but affectionate wit, in his later paintings there is greater sympathy with bourgeois life, but never uncritical sympathy.

Bonnard seldom recorded acts or events. His concern was with the feelings—the ''poetry,'' as he called it—evoked by the things he knew best, and because he favored these subjects, he was even early in his career called an *intimist* painter. But one of the puzzling aspects of Bonnard's art is the detachment in the way the near and the familiar are approached. Often, for example, the people portrayed seem to be only incidentally present in the scene and only remotely conscious of their surroundings. Even the figures given prominence rarely seem

L'Estampe et l'Affiche, poster. (c. 1896).
Color lithograph, 32 x 23 ½″.
The Museum of Modern Art, New York. Purchase

to be aware of the artist or of one another. They are absorbed in themselves, or their attention is averted. This is particularly true of the nudes, sensuously painted as they are. When the attention of an individual is directed toward anything, it is usually toward an animal, a child, or an object. Between adults there is psychological distance, and close physical association only adds an ambiguous tension to it. Bonnard cunningly evokes doubtful and unresolved aspects of human relationship: nostalgia, indifference, wistfulness.

In spite of the initial impression one might get to the contrary, the situations portrayed are not specific. The poses and gestures are the inevitable movements of people doing ordinary things, part of a continuum rather than fixed in crucial moments. With this emphasis on the transient nature of experience is an atmosphere that is hauntingly enigmatic.

The world of Bonnard's art—although it is domestic and pastoral as well as urban—no longer seems to belong to the nineteenth century. It contains too much playful irony and, in later stages, too much melancholy and even apprehensiveness. It shows a range of feeling far wider than that with which it is often credited. Although the choice of imagery seems narrow, the interpretation and expression—the pictorial results—vary the way human feeling itself varies under the slow yet urgent pressures of life.

But while Bonnard may have been passive in his choice of subject, his art was the active, transforming agent of a searching sensibility and mind. He explored color and the effects and clues that determine the perception of both actual and painted objects and nature. In looking at his paintings, especially those done after 1915, one is often initially puzzled by the shape of an object, by an action, or by the definition of space. One has to take time to relate the visual information to physical facts, to associate the disparate painted clues with reality, and to familiarize oneself with the particular conception of each picture—even while on first impression one may be enchanted with the color, amused by the unexpected composition, or as is sometimes the case, disappointed with the whole effect. One readily accepts the familiar subjects with their pleasant associations, but once involved with them one finds that Bonnard also offers new pictorial interpretations of visual experience that push representational art to new limits.

Born in 1867, Bonnard came to artistic maturity in the ebullient, fermenting Paris of the 1890s. As one of the Nabis he was quickly among the avant-garde and was influenced by Gauguin and Japanese art. His association with the Nabis, however, was easygoing, based more on personal friendship than on adherence to any program or militant theory of subject or style. The ideas dominating advanced French painting in the 1890s produced several anti-naturalistic currents with decorative tendencies,

and not unexpectedly, Bonnard's early style belongs to such currents—especially art nouveau. But no matter how decorative his arabesques and flat patterns, Bonnard still infused them with an amazing feeling of playful life and vivid suggestions of personality. That same sense of life he put into every manner in which he worked. He borrowed easily and openly at a time when his fellow artists quarreled fiercely over influences. Bonnard did not worry about reputation; he was too confident in his art.

There were many seeming contradictions in Bonnard. Even in his paintings, facility and elegance of style are combined with a touch that is at times graceless; innocence is combined with sensuousness; the conservative, with the experimental. His pictures offer unconventional perspectives, puzzles, and the surprise of hidden details. In personality he was diffident, but also brilliant, lighthearted, and boyish. Yet in his own unobtrusive way, he remained independent and self-possessed in his art

Place Clichy. (c. 1923). Color lithograph, 18 5/8 x 25 3/16".
Lent by The Art Institute of Chicago

Woman Opening Door. (1941). Pencil, 25½ x 19¾".
Private collection, Paris

Around the beginning of World War I, however, Bonnard seriously questioned the direction in which his interest in nature and impressionism had taken him. He felt he had been carried away by a passion for color and had unconsciously sacrificed form. He began to draw constantly to strengthen form and worked with a new emphasis on composition. At the same time he also developed his use of higher-keyed color, employing it with a renewed sense of the two-dimensional in an unexpected reprise of the decorative aims of his first paintings. The changes that followed took him close to abstraction after 1920 and were based on an unhurried merging of his lyric naturalism with an increasingly monumental decorative goal, which resulted in the spectacular achievements of the last three decades of his life, when he produced his greatest paintings.

Bonnard worked, as he said, with "a brush in one hand, a rag in the other." He did not paint directly from the subject, but from memory, small sketches, and brief color notations. He began with a "first idea," which was usually realized over a long period of time, in a way related to the time required to "read" the finished painting. Angel Zarraga, a Mexican artist who had the opportunity to watch Bonnard at work in a hotel room at Cap d'Antibes, probably during the mid-1920s, gives the following description of Bonnard at work:

> . . . on the walls hung canvases of various sizes and proportions. During my first visit all the canvases were white. The whole room radiated from them. When I came back a few days later, I saw on every one of them a few colorful accents whose pictorial meaning was not at all recognizable. I guessed in part what Bonnard then explained to me. When he begins a picture his composition is not immediately established. . . . He simply walks back and forth between the white surfaces, waits for an idea, sets here a tone, there a brush stroke, puts several streaks on a third canvas. After a little while . . . he lays down his brush, calls his dog, who is always near . . . and goes for a walk with him on the beach. He chats for fifteen minutes or a half hour with acquaintances he meets and then abruptly,

from beginning to end. Although he followed the rapid subsequent changes in French art of his day—fauvism, cubism, dadaism, surrealism, and abstraction—with interest, he remained apart from them. In his own way of painting, however, there was a wide variety at any given time.

Bonnard's evolution also embodied paradoxes. Although in the 1890s he was very much a post-impressionist, he had begun to gravitate toward impressionism before the close of the decade, slowly turning back to a naturalism which he sensed still had unexplored expressive possibilities. After 1900 he paid even more attention to nature, becoming increasingly concerned with space and light, and especially with color. It was then that Bonnard assimilated into his own style technical means of the impressionists—short brush strokes, lighter tonal values, sophisticated hue relationships.

but gently, he breaks off the conversation and returns quickly to his room. Seemingly at random, he sets down here and there, on one picture and another, a few accents which had meanwhile become clear to him and then goes for another walk in order to relax and gather his energies for another attack. Weeks, even months pass in this way. With great astonishment I saw what emerged. . . . Three months later I was again in his room. . . . On the walls I saw half a dozen finished and wonderfully resolved pictures. Before every single one I thought: This was created in a couple of hours, in a hasty mood and with playful ease. 'As for me, I do not know how to invent,' he said to me. He who, one feels, has invented everything! (bibl. 9)

Bonnard was essentially a colorist. He devoted his main creative energies to wedding his sensations of color from nature to those from paint itself—sensations which he said thrilled and even bewildered him. Perceiving color with a highly developed sensitivity, he discovered new and unfamiliar effects from which he selected carefully, yet broadly and audaciously. Sometimes he chose bright, clearly contrasted harmonies of hue, but more often he sought nuances and delicately modulated transitions. Whether in narrow range or multitudinous variety, the colors move across the surface of his paintings in constantly shifting interplay, lending an extraordinary fascination to common subjects. Familiar sights—the pervading greenness of a landscape, the intensification of color in objects on a lightly overcast day—are given vivid life. Sights which escape normal attention are isolated for our pleasure: the detailed changes of planes at the edges of windows are described in many bands of color; shadows cast by objects partially lost in the glare of a strong overhead light are given material substance. New experiences are opened up, as when the chromatic sensations conveyed are like those experienced by mystics or those induced by hallucinatory drugs. As time went on, Bonnard became increasingly daring and original in his use of intense colors and turned it to new expressive ends.

But he did not seek brightness alone. He also worked boldly with contrasts of value—light and dark. Of all the possible combinations of values and colors, he cherished especially the power in combinations of unfamiliar intermediate tones. He used them to record the subtle gradations in a world of half-lights, enhancing them by unexpectedly bright daubs and neighboring tones. In his works irregular juxtapositions of color and tone, ranging from near discordances to tender harmonies, hold the eye entranced. He records the strange illumination just before a storm, the light of predawn and evening: moments of uneasiness, anticipation, and nostalgia. He probed the limits of color experience and discovered wonders seemingly beyond the natural.

Above all, he used his singular effects of light and color to help establish mood. And the moods he cap-

Portrait of Girl. (c. 1942-43). Pencil, 26 x 19¾".
Private collection, Paris

25

Woman in Interior. (1940-41). Pencil, 19 ¾ x 12 ½". Private collection, Paris

tured are incredibly varied—playful, ironic, languorous, enigmatic, joyful, questioning, even exalted —but seldom unmixed. In one of his most important paintings, *Dining Room in the Country* (Page 71), of about 1913, he solves the difficult problem of successfully conveying the extended range of value between interior shadows and full sunlight, and in several ways evokes the equivocal mood. In the painting, a landscape in all the brilliance of a warm day in early summer is seen through an interior, which is also warm, but more shadowed and protected. Within strongly contrasting broad areas of color there is a shimmering play of more closely related hues that increases the sense of light and warmth. The many genre details rendered in an assured but imprecise, painterly way lend the connotations of their presence and unobtrusively build up the sense of comfort and ease, of minor joys and simple pleasures. They are things seen at a glance, or, as the small girl picking flowers, almost unnoticed. The casual position of the brightly dressed woman (probably the artist's wife, Marthe) who leans toward us against the window sill suggests an idle moment and adds to the feeling of indolence that suffuses the picture. She looks at the viewer with a resigned yet vaguely questioning expression, striking a small note of anxiety which reverberates as a muted undercurrent in the comfort of the scene.

It is one of Bonnard's greatest accomplishments that in *Dining Room in the Country* and many other paintings, he goes beyond conveying the experience of observing a scene: he compels the viewer to become a participant. He accomplishes this and the sense of crowding and intimacy, which is achieved even in large scenes, partly through his composition and method of rendering space: he masked or surpressed long diagonals or separate planes which would suggest depth with any precision. As a result, the distant planes with their richly painted surfaces also act as flat shapes close to the picture plane. Paradoxically, then, the elements which imply recession into space tend to compress space and to augment the sense of a closed and intimate scene. Soon after painting the *Dining Room in the Country* Bonnard began using mirrors frequently, and even mirrors within mirrors, in a similar way to limit the depth of a picture and at the same time to lead even further into space. By cutting off objects in the foreground of his paintings (usually at the lower edge of the composition, sometimes at the side and top) he also brought a scene close. Table tops, for instance, often seem to continue beyond the lower edge of the picture, and one feels a sharp drop into space where they have been cut off.

Bonnard's extraordinary power to communicate is also strengthened by the unorthodox points of view that he chose. These were not just matters of whim, although a lot of whimsy is behind them. He was using parts of the field of vision audaciously and boldly to ferret out and underline mood. *The Table* (Page 47), of 1925, for example, is painted throughout with equal attention and emphasis. The objects in the large still life are defined with summary brilliance and spread out on a long table. Yet surprisingly, as one looks at the picture there is a growing awareness that the still life, although it occupies more than half the picture, is dominated by the small figure of Marthe in the left background. The emphasis wavers, but the figure seems to hover over the foreground with a strange persistence. This is not only because Marthe is seen almost from eye level, it is also because Bonnard did not move his viewpoint from side to side: the numerous other things are seen from vantage points that fluctuate in height, but which are all ranged along a vertical line almost directly in front of the figure of Marthe. It is unconventional, too, that *The Table* is painted as if seen entirely in the right half of the artist's field of vision. His eye is focused on Marthe, and the other objects in the picture seem to be only incidentally seen as he glanced at her, so quickly we are not even sure of her action. (One gains the impression, however, that she is preparing food for the dog whose snout seems to be shown near her at the left.)

Standing Nude. (c. 1900). Charcoal, 16 ½ x 9 ¾".
The Metropolitan Museum of Art, New York, Dick Fund, 1948

Garden at Vernon. (1915-20). Pen and ink and pencil, 9 ¾ x 12 ½".
Private collection, Paris

Such manipulation of the field of vision has not been uncommon among modern painters; but of those who used it, Bonnard was among the most venturesome and put the greatest strain on the conventions of academic perspective. Frequently he extended the field of vision to an extremely wide angle. This brought about the linear "distortions" and undulations so often noted in his work. The eye actually sees things in this way, Bonnard insisted. And so it does, but in peripheral vision where one is seldom consciously aware of the sensation. Nonetheless, this kind of vision, even though it operates outside clear focus, is an essential part of sight, acting as the framing, enclosing factor. In utilizing the disparities between the normal view and academically accepted means of representing a scene, on the one hand, and the actual experience of seeing, on the other, Bonnard usually exploited the psychological as well as formal implications. He used them to control attention and feeling within a picture: things

in focus seem to be closer and have more presence; things in the margin of vision are seen, so to speak, blankly, with a certain shyness and detachment.

Seeing Bonnard's paintings in number is like reading entries in a journal by a master of indirect statement. That he took his subjects from his private environment is another modern facet of his art. Just as landscape grew from an incidental element to the rank of major subject in the past, so an artists' personal environment became an increasingly important subject after impressionism. Few other painters seem to have remained content to choose motifs from within such a narrow compass, and very few painters could have wrested such incredible variety from these motifs. There was no need, nor did Bonnard find, a place in his art for the exotic or frankly dramatic subject.

While he moved back and forth between relatively conservative and outspokenly radical methods of representation, the evolution of his art as a whole tends toward the latter pole: color breaks increasingly away from nature; the vantage point at times becomes so eccentric that the resulting image lies practically outside visual illusion; architectural settings shift so that almost every clue by which the spectator can orient himself is dissembled. In a known and ostensibly enjoyable world, Bonnard withholds certainty as to many identities—identities of subject, position, human reaction. The plausible is rendered implausible. He asks new questions about the relation between what we experience and that which actually exists in nature and in art. Moreover, he unconsciously anticipated the latest revolutionary discoveries of the science of perception, which have led to practical application in such things as wide-screen film techniques dependent on peripheral vision to give the viewer a sometimes uncanny sense of actual participation in what is shown. Although he chose not to participate in the more abstract tendencies of his time, these searchings and probings took Bonnard ever closer to abstraction. His approach to it was unprogrammed and came unbidden out of the very logic of his essentially representational art; it was, therefore, all the more organic and natural.

Greater understanding of Bonnard's art has contributed importantly to the critical rehabilitation of late impressionism that has taken place in the past two decades. Appreciation of his art has helped prepare us for the renewed appreciation of Monet. Nonetheless, Bonnard was no mere disciple of impressionism and is far from an anachronism in twentieth-century art. His affiliations with impressionism led some critics to characterize him as a conservative if brilliant artist; and indeed he was conservative in certain respects. But that he was not essentially so, that he remained abreast of the most advanced art of his time in other and more crucial respects, was too often overlooked. His return and adherence to nature in a period that produced fauvism, cubism, and pure abstraction had looked like a retreat. It has proven, instead to be another instance of *reculer pour mieux sauter*—of stepping back to leap further. Bonnard's "naturalism" became a springboard for dazzling innovations through which he rejoined the main tradition of his time, enriched it, and assumed a place in the highest rank of its artists.

JAMES ELLIOTT

Children Leaving School. (c. 1893). Tempera, 11 ⅜ x 17 ½". Collection Lauder Greenway, New York

The Cottet Family. 1894. Oil, 13 ¾ x 10 ⅝". M. Knoedler & Co., Inc., New York

Screen (*Promenade des nourrices, frise des fiacres*). (c.1892-94). Distemper; four panels, each 58 x 17 ¾". Private collection, New York

Roof Tops. (c.1895-1900). Oil, 13 ½ x 15″. Smith College Museum of Art, Northampton, Massachusetts. Gift of The Adele R. Levy Fund, Inc.

Street Scene with Two Dogs (*Rue à Éragny-sur-Oise*). (1895). Oil, 13 ⅞ x 10 ⅝″. Collection Mr. and Mrs. Jacques Gelman, Mexico City

OPPOSITE: *The Bridge at Chatou.* (c. 1896). Oil, 12 ½ x 23 ½″. Private collection, New York

Madame Terrasse and Her Children. 1898. Oil,
13 x 10½". Collection Mrs. Mellon Bruce, New York

Place Blanche. (c.1902). Oil, 23½ x 31¼". Collection Edward G. Robinson, Los Angeles

OPPOSITE: *Les Champs-Elysées.* (c. 1898). Oil, 20½ x 30". Private collection, Lausanne

Girl in a Straw Hat. (1903). Oil, 15 x 17½". Milwaukee Art Center Collection. Gift of Harry Lynde Bradley

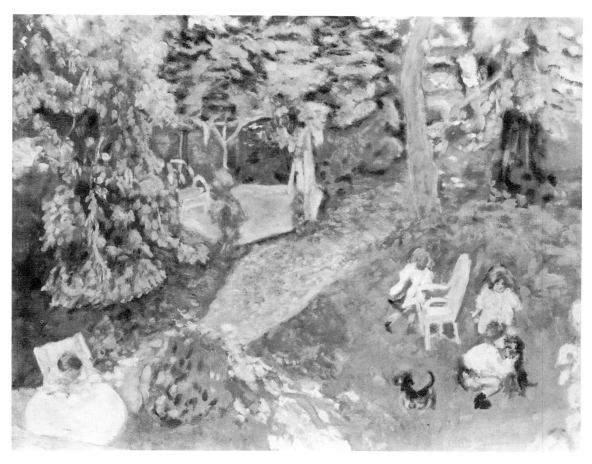

Children in Garden. (1908). Oil, 19 x 25″. Collection Mr. and Mrs. Lester Avnet, Kings Point, New York

OPPOSITE: *Repas des bêtes*. (C.1906). Oil, 29 x 42″. Collection Mr. and Mrs. Hugo Moser, New York

Regatta. (1908-12). Oil, 28 ⅝ x 39 ¾″. Museum of Art, Carnegie Institute, Pittsburgh

OPPOSITE: *Tree near the River.* (C.1912). Oil, 40 x 31 ¾″. Sonja Henie's and Niels Onstad's Collection, Los Angeles

Woman with Basket of Fruit. (1915-18). Oil, 26 ¾ x 15 ⅝". The Baltimore
Museum of Art, Cone Collection

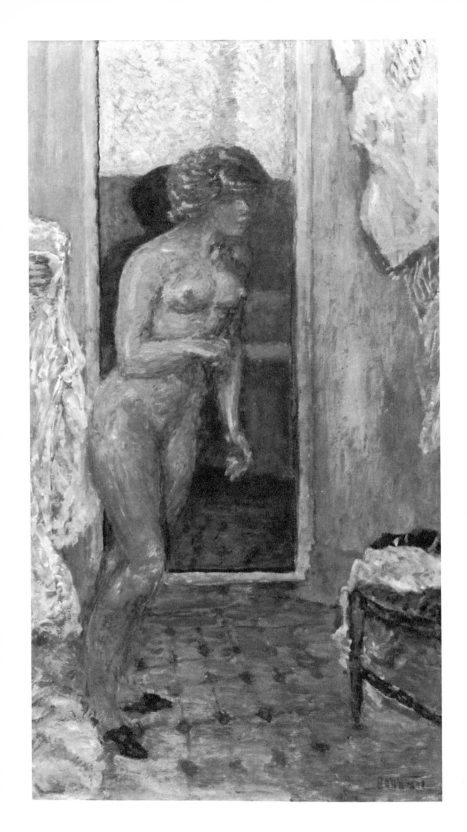

Nude Leaving Bath. (1915). Oil, 48 ¼ x 25 ⅝".
Collection Mr. and Mrs. Jacques Gelman, Mexico City

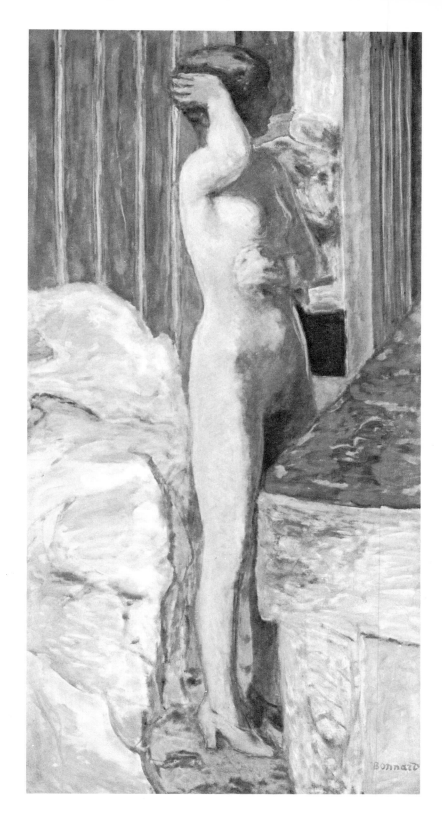

Standing Nude. (1930). Oil, 49 ¼ x 25 ¼″. Collection
Mr. and Mrs. John D. Rockefeller 3rd, New York

Interior with Woman in Wicker Chair. 1920. Oil, 28 ⅜ x 20 ⅛". Nationalmuseum, Stockholm

OPPOSITE: *Flowers on Chimney Piece.* (1913). Oil, 32 x 21 ½". Collection Mr. and Mrs. William Goetz, Los Angeles

Still Life with Basket of Bananas. (1923). Oil, 23 ¾ x 25 ⅜". Collection Mr. and Mrs. Jacques Gelman, Mexico City

OPPOSITE: *Nude Bending Forward.* (C.1923). Oil, 41 ⅜ x 33 ⅛". Private collection, New York

OPPOSITE: *The Table.* (1925). 40 ½ x 29 ¼″. The Trustees of The Tate Gallery, London

LEFT: *Still Life (La Table garnie).* (c.1924). Oil, 15 x 22″. The Art Gallery of Toronto

The Dining Room at Le Cannet. (1924). Oil, 24 x 22 ½″. Collection Mr. and Mrs. Clifford W. Michel, New York

Bouquet at Vernon. (c.1925). Watercolor, 25 ⅝ x 19 ⅝″. Private collection, New York

46

Self-Portrait. (c.1926). Oil, 20 ⅞ x 14 ⅛″. Private collection, New York

Self-Portrait. (1938). Oil, 23 x 26 ⅜″. Private collection, New York

LEFT: *The Three Bouquets.* (1930). Oil, 22 ¾ x 23 ½".
Collection Mr. and Mrs. André Meyer, New York

Baskets of Fruit in Sun. (c.1927). Oil, 23 ¾ x 17 ¼".
Collection Mr. and Mrs. Theodore E. Cummings,
Beverly Hills, California

Landscape (La Grande vue de Vernon). (1929). Oil, 42 ¼ x 51 ½". Collection Mr. and Mrs. Alex M. Lewyt, New York

Tugboat at Vernon. (c.1929). Oil, 22 ½ x 24 ⅛". Collection Mr. and Mrs. Charles W. Engelhard, Far Hills, New Jersey

OPPOSITE: *Landscape of the Midi.* (c.1930). Oil, 24 ¾ x 31 ⅞". Smith College Museum of Art, Northampton, Massachusetts

The Road to Nantes. (c. 1930). Oil, 27 ¼ x 25 ⅞″. The Cleveland Museum of Art, Leonard C. Hanna, Jr. Collection

OPPOSITE: *Bowl of Fruit.* (c. 1933). Oil, 22 ¾ x 20 ¾″. Philadelphia Museum of Art, Lisa Norris Elkins Collection

Dining Room on the Garden. (c.1933). Oil, 50 ⅛ x 53 ½″. The Solomon R. Guggenheim Museum, New York

OPPOSITE: *Table with Music Album.* (1926-32). Oil, 47 ¾ x 35 ¾″. Private collection, New York

The Breakfast Table. (c.1935). Oil, 25 ¼ x 37 ½". Collection Mr. and Mrs. William B. Jaffe, New York

Landscape, Le Cannet. (1938). Oil, 20 ¾ x 28 ¾".
Collection Mrs. Walter Ross, New York

Peaches and Grapes. (c.1938-40). Oil, 19 x 13 ⅜″.
Wildenstein & Co., Inc., New York

The Dessert. (c.1940). Oil, 18 ¼ x 25 ⅝″. Sonja
Henie's and Niels Onstad's Collection, Los Angeles

Table before Window. (1943). Oil, 40 x 28 ½″. Collection Edward A. Bragaline, New York

OPPOSITE: *View from Window.* (c. 1936-38). Crayon, 13 x 19 ¼″. Private collection, New York

The Sea. (c.1944). Watercolor, 11 x 10¼".
Private collection, New York

COLOR PLATES

Woman with Rabbit. 1891. Oil, 37 ¾ x 17".
Collection Professor William Rubin, New York

The Croquet Game. 1892. Oil, 50 ¾ x 63 ½". Private collection, Paris

OPPOSITE: *Interior.* (1898). Oil, 20 ½ x 13 ¾". Collection Mr. and Mrs. Norton Simon, Los Angeles

Boulevard des Batignolles. (1900). Oil, 11 ⅝ x 15 ¾". Collection Mrs. Mellon Bruce, New York

The Bridge. (c. 1908). Oil, 27 x 38″. Collection Mr. and Mrs. Sidney F. Brody, Los Angeles

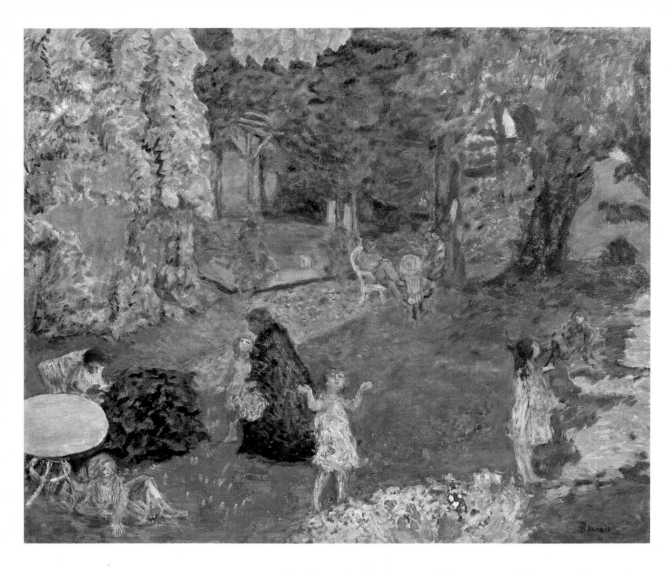

The Terrasse Family. (c.1904). Oil, 42 ½ x 49 ⅝". Private collection, Paris

OPPOSITE: *Dining Room in the Country, Vernon*. 1913. Oil, 64 ½ x 80". The Minneapolis Institute of Arts

Nude Resting. (1927). Oil, 42 ½ x 56". Wildenstein & Co., Inc., New York

OPPOSITE: *Interior with Flowers.* (1924). Oil, 16 x 35 ½". Collection Mr. and Mrs. Walter Bareiss

OPPOSITE: *The Brothers Jean and Gaston Bernheim.* 1920. Oil, 65 x 61″. Musée National d'Art Moderne, Paris

Dressing Table and Mirror. (c.1920). Oil, 48 ⅞ x 43″. Collection Mr. and Mrs. Gustave M. Berne, Great Neck, N. Y.

74

St. Honoré-les-Bains. (1924). Oil, 20½ x 30½". Collection Mr. and Mrs. John D. Rockefeller 3rd, New York

OPPOSITE: *The Palm*. 1926. Oil, 44 x 57½". The Phillips Collection, Washington, D. C.

OPPOSITE: *Red Poppies*. (1926). Oil, 29 ⅛ x 16 ½". Collection Mr. and Mrs. Jacques Gelman, Mexico City

Grapes. (c.1928). Oil, 16 ⅝ x 18 ¼". Collection James Thrall Soby, New Canaan, Connecticut

The Seine at Vernon. (1930). Oil, 42 ½ x 42 ½″. The Art Institute of Chicago, Clyde M. Carr Fund

OPPOSITE: *The Breakfast Room.* (C.1930-31). Oil, 62 ⅞ x 44 ⅞″. The Museum of Modern Art, N. Y., given anonymously

OPPOSITE: *Terrace at Vernon (Decor à Vernon).* (c. 1930-38). Oil, 58 x 75½". Collection Mrs. Frank J. Gould, Cannes

Breakfast. (c.1930). Oil, 17½ x 22". Collection Mrs. Lloyd Bruce Wescott, Rosemont, New Jersey

84

Nude in Bathroom (Cabinet de toilette). (1932). Oil, 47 ½ x 46 ¼". Collection Mrs. Wolfgang Schoenborn, New York

Landscape of the Midi. (c. 1935). Oil, 39 ¼ x 49 ½". Collection Wright Ludington, Santa Barbara, California

Mediterranean Coast. (c.1943). Oil, 37 ¾ x 28 ½″. The Lazarus Phillips Family Collection, Montreal

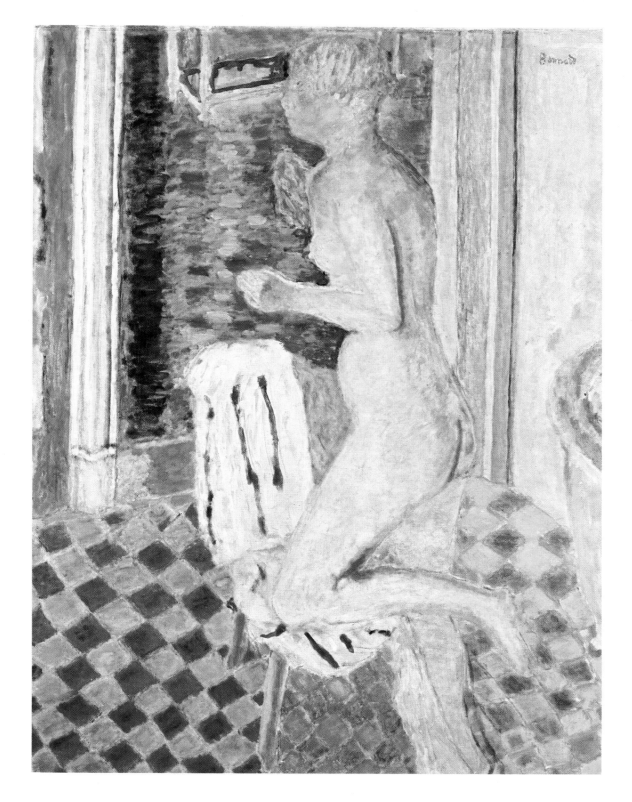

Nude and Chair. (c. 1936-38). Oil, 50 x 33″. Collection Mr. znd Mrs. Charles Zadok, New York

OPPOSITE: *Nude in Bathtub*. (c.1938-41). Oil, 48 x 59 ½". Collection Mr. and Mrs. Charles Zadok, New York

The Yellow Boat. (c.1936-38). Oil, 22 ¾ x 29 ⅞". Collection Mr. and Mrs. Charles Zadok, New York

View from the Terrace (*La Terrasse ensoleillée*). (c.1939). Oil, 28 x 93″. Private collection, Paris

The Pedicure. (1936). Oil, 20 ½ x 32 ¾″. Collection Silvan Kocher, Solothurn, Switzerland

OPPOSITE: *Nude in Yellow (Le Grand nu jaune).* (1938-40?). Oil, 67 x 42 ½″. Private collection, New York

Still Life (Coin de table). (c.1935). Oil, 26 ⅜ x 25″. Musée National d'Art Moderne, Paris

The Bottle of Red Wine. 1942. Oil, 26 x 24″. Collection Mr. and Mrs. Ralph F. Colin, New York

Self-Portrait. (1940). Oil, 30¼ x 24½″. Wildenstein & Co., Inc., New York

Self-Portrait. (1945). Oil, 22 x 18". Collection Mr. and Mrs. Donald S. Stralem, New York

View from the Studio, Le Cannet. (1945). Oil, 37 x 49". Milwaukee Art Center Collection. Gift of Harry Lynde Bradley

The Studio at Le Cannet, with Mimosa. (1938-46). Oil, 50 x 50″. Private collection, France

102

OPPOSITE: *The Garden*. (c. 1935).
Oil, 50 x 39 ⅜".
Musée du Petit Palais, Paris

Morning: The Open Door. (c.1937).
Oil, 49 ⅝ x 28".
Private collection, Paris

Basket of Fruit. (c.1946). Oil, 34 x 28″. The Reader's Digest Association, Pleasantville, New York

Flowering Almond Tree. (1946).
Oil, 21 ⅝ x 14 ⅜".
Musée National d'Art Moderne, Paris

LENDERS TO THE EXHIBITION:

Mr. and Mrs. Lester Avnet, Kings Point, New York; Roland Balaÿ, New York; Mr. and Mrs. Walter Bareiss; Mr. and Mrs. Gustave M. Berne, Great Neck, New York; Mr. and Mrs. Leigh B. Block, Chicago; Edward A. Bragaline, New York; Mr. and Mrs. Sidney F. Brody, Los Angeles; Mrs. Mellon Bruce, New York; Mr. and Mrs. Ralph F. Colin, New York; Mr. and Mrs. Theodore E. Cummings, Beverly Hills, California; Mr. and Mrs. Seth Dennis, Westport, Connecticut; Mr. and Mrs. Charles W. Engelhard, Far Hills, New Jersey; Mr. and Mrs. Jacques Gelman, Mexico City; Mr. and Mrs. William Goetz, Los Angeles; Lauder Greenway, New York; Mrs. Frank J. Gould, Cannes; Mr. and Mrs. William B. Jaffe, New York; Silvan Kocher, Solothurn, Switzerland; Mr. and Mrs. Alex M. Lewyt, New York; Wright Ludington, Santa Barbara, California; Mr. and Mrs. André Meyer, New York; Mr. and Mrs. Clifford W. Michel, New York; Mr. and Mrs. Hugo Moser, New York; Sonja Henie's and Neils Onstad's Collection, Los Angeles; The Lazarus Phillips Family Collection, Montreal; The Reader's Digest Association, Pleasantville, New York; Edward G. Robinson, Los Angeles; Mr. and Mrs. John D. Rockefeller 3rd, New York; Mrs. Walter Ross, New York; Professor William Rubin, New York; Mrs. Wolfgang Schoenborn, New York; Mr. and Mrs. Norton Simon, Los Angeles; James Thrall Soby, New Canaan, Connecticut; Mr. and Mrs. Donald S. Stralem, New York; Mrs. Lloyd Bruce Wescott, Rosemont, New Jersey; Mr. and Mrs. Charles Zadok, New York

The Baltimore Museum of Art; The Art Institute of Chicago; The Cleveland Museum of Art; The Tate Gallery, London; Milwaukee Art Center; The Minneapolis Institute of Arts; The Solomon R. Guggenheim Museum, New York; The Metropolitan Museum of Art, New York; The Museum of Modern Art, New York; Smith College Museum of Art, Northampton, Massachusetts; Musée National d'Art Moderne, Paris; Musée du Petit Palais, Paris; Philadelphia Museum of Art; Museum of Art, Carnegie Institute, Pittsburgh; Nationalmuseum, Stockholm; The Art Gallery of Toronto; Galleria Internazionale d'Arte Moderna, Venice; The Phillips Collection, Washington, D.C.

M. Knoedler & Co., Inc., New York; Frank Perls Gallery, Beverly Hills, California; Wildenstein & Co., Inc., New York.

CATALOGUE OF THE EXHIBITION

The Museum of Modern Art, New York:
October 7—November 29, 1964
The Art Institute of Chicago:
January 8—February 28, 1965
Los Angeles County Museum of Art:
March 31—May 30, 1965

Bonnard himself attached little importance to dates, as he sometimes worked on a picture over a period of many years; therefore, it is impossible to date many of his works with any degree of assurance. Discrepancies as wide as fifteen years exist between the estimates of the most informed students. We have, therefore, listed the dates commonly agreed upon, even though future research will inevitably alter certain of them.

Dates in parentheses do not appear on the work. In dimensions height precedes width.

PAINTINGS

1. *Woman with Rabbit*. 1891. Oil on canvas, 37¾ x 17″. Collection Professor William Rubin, New York. Ill. p. 65.

2. *The Croquet Game*. 1892. Oil on canvas, 50¾ x 63½″. Private collection, Paris. Ill. p. 66.

3. *Screen (Promenade des nourrices, frise des fiacres)*. (c. 1892-94). Distemper on unprimed canvas; four panels, each 58 x 17¾″. Private collection, New York. Ill. p. 31.

4. *Children Leaving School*. (c.1893). Tempera on cardboard, 11⅜ x 17½″. Collection Lauder Greenway, New York. Ill. p. 30.

5. *The Cottet Family*. 1894. Oil on wood, 13¾ x 10⅝″. M. Knoedler & Co., Inc., New York. Ill. p. 30.

6. *Street Scene with Two Dogs (Rue à Éragny-sur-Oise)*. (1895). Oil on composition board, 13⅞ x 10⅝″. Collection Mr. and Mrs. Jacques Gelman, Mexico City. Ill. p. 32.

7. *Roof Tops*. (c.1895-1900). Oil on cardboard, 13½ x 15″. Smith College Museum of Art, Northampton, Massachusetts. Gift of The Adele R. Levy Fund, Inc. Ill. p. 32.

8. *The Bridge at Chatou*. (c.1896). Oil on wood, 12½ x 23½″. Private collection, New York. Ill. p. 33.

9. *Madame Terrasse and Her Children*. 1898. Oil on cardboard, mounted on wood, 13 x 10½″. Collection Mrs. Mellon Bruce, New York. Ill. p. 33.

10. *Interior*. (1898). Oil on cardboard, 20½ x 13¾″. Collection Mr. and Mrs. Norton Simon, Los Angeles. Ill. p. 67.

11. *Les Champs-Elysées*. (c.1898). Oil on board, 20½ x 30″. Private collection, Lausanne. Ill. p. 35.

12. *Boulevard des Batignolles*. (1900). Oil on wood, 11⅝ x 15¾″. Collection Mrs. Mellon Bruce, New York. Ill. p. 68.

13. *Place Blanche*. (c.1902). Oil on paper, mounted on wood, 23½ x 31¼″. Collection Edward G. Robinson, Los Angeles. Ill. p. 34.

14. *Girl in a Straw Hat*. (1903). Oil on canvas, 15 x 17½″. Milwaukee Art Center Collection. Gift of Harry Lynde Bradley. Ill. p. 35.

15. *The Terrasse Family*. (c.1904). Oil on canvas, 42½ x 49⅝″. Private collection, Paris. Ill. p. 70.

16. *Repas des bêtes*. (c.1906). Oil on canvas, 29 x 42″. Collection Mr. and Mrs. Hugo Moser, New York. Ill. p. 36.

17. *The Bridge*. (c.1908). Oil on canvas, 27 x 38″. Collection Mr. and Mrs. Sidney F. Brody, Los Angeles. Ill. p. 69.

18. *Children in Garden*. (1908). Oil on canvas, 19 x 25″. Col-

lection Mr. and Mrs. Lester Avnet, Kings Point, New York. Ill. p. 37.

19. *Regatta.* (1908-12). Oil on canvas, 25⅝ x 39¾". Museum of Art, Carnegie Institute, Pittsburgh. Ill. p. 38.

20. *Tree near the River.* (c.1912). Oil on canvas, 40 x 31¾". Sonja Henie's and Niels Onstad's Collection, Los Angeles. Ill. p. 39.

21. *Dining Room in the Country, Vernon.* 1913. Oil on canvas, 64½ x 80". The Minneapolis Institute of Arts. Ill. p. 71 and cover.

22. *Flowers on Chimney Piece.* (1913). Oil on canvas, 32 x 21½". Collection Mr. and Mrs. William Goetz, Los Angeles. Ill. p. 43.

23. *Nude Leaving Bath.* (1915). Oil on canvas, 48¼ x 25⅝". Collection Mr. and Mrs. Jacques Gelman, Mexico City. Ill. p. 40.

24. *Woman with Basket of Fruit.* (1915-18). Oil on canvas, 26¾ x 15⅝". The Baltimore Museum of Art, Cone Collection. Ill. p. 39.

25. *The Brothers Jean and Gaston Bernheim.* 1920. Oil on canvas, 65 x 61". Musée National d'Art Moderne, Paris. Ill. p. 75.

26. *Interior with Woman in Wicker Chair.* 1920. Oil on canvas, 28⅜ x 20⅛". Nationalmuseum, Stockholm. Ill. p. 42.

27. *Dressing Table and Mirror.* (c.1920). Oil on canvas, 48⅞ x 43". Collection Mr. and Mrs. Gustave M. Berne, Great Neck, New York. Ill. p. 74.

28. *Still Life with Basket of Bananas.* (1923). Oil on canvas, 23¾ x 25⅜". Collection Mr. and Mrs. Jacques Gelman, Mexico City. Ill. p. 44.

29. *Nude Bending Forward.* (c.1923). Oil on canvas, 41⅜ x 33⅛". Private collection, New York. Ill. p. 45.

30. *St. Honoré-les-Bains.* (1924). Oil on canvas, 20½ x 30½". Collection Mr. and Mrs. John D. Rockefeller 3rd, New York. Ill. p. 76.

31. *Still Life (La Table garnie).* (c.1924). Oil on canvas, 15 x 22". The Art Gallery of Toronto. Ill. p. 46.

32. *Interior with Flowers.* (1924). Oil on canvas, 45⅞ x 35½". Collection Mr. and Mrs. Walter Bareiss. Ill. p. 72.

33. *The Dining Room at Le Cannet.* (1924). Oil on canvas, 24 x 22½". Collection Mr. and Mrs. Clifford W. Michel, New York. Ill. p. 46.

34. *The Table.* (1925). Oil on canvas, 40½ x 29¼". The Trustees of The Tate Gallery, London. Ill. p. 47.

35. *The Green Slipper.* (c.1925). Oil on canvas, 56 x 32". Collection Mr. and Mrs. Leigh B. Block, Chicago. Ill. p. 84.

36. *Bouquet at Vernon.* (c.1925). Watercolor, 25⅝ x 19⅜". Private collection, New York. Ill. p. 46.

37. *The Palm.* 1926. Oil on canvas, 44 x 57½". The Phillips Collection, Washington, D. C. Ill. p. 77.

38. *Red Poppies.* (1926). Oil on canvas, 29⅛ x 16½". Collection Mr. and Mrs. Jacques Gelman, Mexico City. Ill. p. 79.

39. *Self-Portrait.* (c.1926). Oil on canvas, 20⅞ x 14⅛". Private collection, New York. Ill. p. 48.

40. *Table with Music Album.* (1926-32). Oil on canvas, 47¾ x 35¾". Private collection, New York. Ill. p. 57.

41. *Nude Resting.* (1927). Oil on canvas, 42½ x 56". Wildenstein & Co., Inc., New York. Ill. p. 73.

42. *Baskets of Fruit in Sun.* (c.1927). Oil on canvas, 23¾ x 17¼". Collection Mr. and Mrs. Theodore E. Cummings, Beverly Hills, California. Ill. p. 50.

43. *Grapes.* (c.1928). Oil on canvas, 16⅝ x 18¼". Collection James Thrall Soby, New Canaan, Connecticut. Ill. p. 78.

44. *Landscape (La Grande vue de Vernon).* (1929). Oil on canvas, 42¼ x 51½". Collection Mr. and Mrs. Alex M. Lewyt. New York. Ill. p. 51.

45. *Tugboat at Vernon.* (c. 1929). Oil on canvas, 22½ x 24⅛". Collection Mr. and Mrs. Charles W. Engelhard, Far Hills, New Jersey. Ill. p. 52.

46. *The Three Bouquets.* (1930). Oil on canvas, 22¾ x 23½". Collection Mr. and Mrs. André Meyer, New York. Ill. p. 50.

47. *The Seine at Vernon.* (1930). Oil on canvas, 42½ x 42½". The Art Institute of Chicago, Clyde M. Carr Fund. Ill. p. 80.

48. *Landscape of the Midi.* (c.1930). Oil on canvas, 24¾ x 31⅞". Smith College Museum of Art, Northampton, Massachusetts. Ill. p. 53.

49. *Breakfast.* (c. 1930). Oil on canvas, 17½ x 22". Collection Mrs. Lloyd Bruce Wescott, Rosemont, New Jersey. Ill. p. 82.

50. *The Road to Nantes.* (c.1930). Oil on canvas, 27¼ x 25⅞". The Cleveland Museum of Art, Leonard C. Hanna, Jr. Collection. Ill. p. 54.

51. *Standing Nude.* (c.1930). Oil on canvas, 49¼ x 25¼". Collection Mr. and Mrs. John D. Rockefeller 3rd, New York. Ill. p. 41.

52. *The Breakfast Room.* (c.1930-31). Oil on canvas, 62⅞ x 44⅞". The Museum of Modern Art, New York, given anonymously. Ill. p. 81.

53. *Terrace at Vernon (Decor à Vernon).* (c. 1930-38). Oil on canvas, 58 x 75½". Collection Mrs. Frank J. Gould, Cannes. Ill. p. 83.

54. *Nude in Bathroom (Cabinet de toilette).* (1932). Oil on canvas, 47½ x 46¼". Collection Mrs. Wolfgang Schoenborn, New York. Ill. p. 85.

55. *Nude before a Mirror.* (1933). Oil on canvas, 59⅞ x 40⅛". Galleria Internazionale d'Arte Moderna, Venice. Ill. p. 87.

56. *Bowl of Fruit.* (c.1933). Oil on canvas, 22¾ x 20¾". Philadelphia Museum of Art, Lisa Norris Elkins Collection. Ill. p. 55.

57. *Dining Room on the Garden.* (c.1933). Oil on canvas, 50⅛ x 53½". The Solomon R. Guggenheim Museum, New York. Ill. p. 56.

58. *The Breakfast Table.* (c.1935). Oil on canvas, 25¼ x 37½". Collection Mr. and Mrs. William B. Jaffe, New York. Ill. p. 58.

59. *Landscape of the Midi.* (c.1935). Oil on canvas, 39¼ x 49½". Collection Wright Ludington, Santa Barbara, California. Ill. p. 86.

60. *Still Life (Coin de table).* (c.1935). Oil on canvas, 26⅜ x 25". Musée National d'Art Moderne, Paris. Ill. p. 96.

61. *The Garden.* (c.1935). Oil on canvas, 50 x 39⅜. Musée du Petit Palais, Paris. Ill. p. 102.

62. *The Pedicure.* (1936). Oil on canvas, 20½ x 32¾". Collection Silvan Kocher, Solothurn, Switzerland. Ill. p. 94.

63. *The Yellow Boat.* (c.1936-38). Oil on canvas, 22¾ x 29⅞". Collection Mr. and Mrs. Charles Zadok, New York. Ill. p. 90.

64. *Nude and Chair.* (c.1936-38). Oil on canvas, 50 x 33". Collection Mr. and Mrs. Charles Zadok, New York. Ill. p. 89.

65. *Morning: The Open Door.* (c. 1937). Oil on canvas, 49⅝ x 28". Private collection, Paris. Ill. p. 103.

66. *Self-Portrait.* (1938). Oil on canvas, 23 x 26⅜". Private collection, New York. Ill. p. 49.

67. *Landscape, Le Cannet.* (1938). Oil on canvas, 20¾ x 28¾". Collection Mrs. Walter Ross, New York. Ill. p. 58.

68. *Mediterranean Coast.* (c.1943). Oil on canvas, 37¾ x 28½". The Lazarus Phillips Family Collection, Montreal. Ill. p. 88.

69. *Nude in Yellow (Le Grand nu jaune).* (1938-40?). Oil on canvas, 67 x 42½". Private collection, New York. Ill. p. 95.

70. *Peaches and Grapes.* (c.1938-40). Oil on canvas, 19 x 13⅜". Wildenstein & Co., Inc., New York. Ill. p. 59.

71. *Nude in Bathtub.* (c.1938-41). Oil on canvas, 48 x 59½". Collection Mr. and Mrs. Charles Zadok, New York. Ill. p. 91.

72. *The Studio at Le Cannet, with Mimosa.* (1938-46). Oil on canvas, 50 x 50". Private collection, France. Ill. p. 101.

73. *View from the Terrace (La Terrasse ensoleillée).* (c.1939). Oil on canvas, 28 x 93". Private collection, Paris. Ill. p. 92-93.

74. *Self-Portrait.* (1940). Oil on canvas, 30¼ x 24½". Wildenstein & Co., Inc., New York. Ill. p. 98.

75. *The Dessert.* (c.1940). Oil on canvas, 18¼ x 25⅝". Sonja Henie's and Niels Onstad's Collection, Los Angeles. Ill. p. 59.

76. *The Bottle of Red Wine.* 1942. Oil on canvas, 26 x 24". Collection Mr. and Mrs. Ralph F. Colin, New York. Ill. p. 97.

77. *Table before Window.* (1943). Oil on canvas, 40 x 28½". Collection Edward A. Bragaline, New York. Ill. p. 60.

78. *Still Life with Fruit.* (c.1943-44). Oil on canvas, 26½ x 21½". Private collection, New York. Ill. p. 104.

79. *The Sea.* (c.1944). Watercolor, 11 x 10¼". Private collection, New York. Ill. p. 61.

80. *Self-Portrait.* (1945). Oil on canvas, 22 x 18". Collection Mr. and Mrs. Donald S. Stralem, New York. Ill. p. 99.

81. *View from the Studio, Le Cannet.* (1945). Oil on canvas, 37 x 49". Milwaukee Art Center Collection. Gift of Harry Lynde Bradley. Ill. p. 100.

82. *Basket of Fruit.* (c.1946). Oil on canvas, 34 x 28". The Reader's Digest Association, Pleasantville, New York. Ill. p. 105.

83. *Flowering Almond Tree.* (1946). Oil on canvas, 21⅝ x 14⅜". Musée National d'Art Moderne, Paris. Ill. p. 106.

DRAWINGS

84. *Parade Ground.* (1889). Pen and ink, 7⅞ x 11¹³⁄₁₆". Collection Roland Balaÿ, New York.

85. *Girls.* (c. 1893). Pen and ink, 10 x 14". Frank Perls Gallery, Beverly Hills, California. Ill. p. 9.

86. *Municipal Guard.* (1893). Brush, pen and ink, pencil, 15¾ x 11¾". Private collection, Paris.

87. *Girl in Profile.* (1894). Charcoal, 12¼ x 7¾". Private collection, Paris.

88. *Laundry Girl.* (1896). Charcoal, 12¼ x 7¾". Private collection, Paris. Ill. p. 20.

89. *Standing Nude.* (c.1900). Charcoal, 16½ x 9¾". The Metropolitan Museum of Art, New York, Dick Fund, 1948. Ill. p. 27.

90. *Standing Nude, Back.* (c.1900-05). Charcoal, 12½ x 9½". Private collection, Paris.

91. *Cat,* illustration for *Histoires Naturelles* (p. 75). (1904). Brush and ink, 12⅛ x 7⅜". Collection Mr. and Mrs. Seth Dennis, Westport, Connecticut.

92. *Rooster,* illustration for *Histoires Naturelles* (p. 26). (1904). Brush and ink, 12 x 7¾". Collection Mr. and Mrs. Seth Dennis, Westport, Connecticut.

93. *Swan,* illustration for *Histoires Naturelles* (p. 65). (1904). Brush and ink, 12⅛ x 7½". Collection Mr. and Mrs. Seth Dennis, Westport, Connecticut. Ill. p. 15.

94. *Study of Seated Nude and Hands.* (c.1913). Charcoal, 22¾ x 17¼". Private collection, Paris.

95. *Garden at Vernon.* (1915-20). Pen and ink and pencil, 9¾ x 12½". Private collection, Paris. Ill. p. 28.

96. *Bending Nude in Bathtub.* (c.1930-35). Pencil 9½ x 12¼". Private collection, Paris.

97. *Bending Nude in Profile.* (1930-35). Pencil, 12½ x 9½". Private collection, Paris.

98. *View from Window.* (c.1936-38). Crayon, 13 x 19¼". Private collection, New York. Ill. p. 61.

99. *Woman in Interior.* (1940-41). Pencil, 19¾ x 12½". Private collection, Paris. Ill. p. 26.

100. *Woman Opening Door.* (1941). Pencil, 25½ x 19¾". Private collection, Paris. Ill. p. 24.

101. *Portrait of Girl.* (c.1942-43). Pencil, 26 x 19¾". Private collection, Paris. Ill. p. 25.

102. *View from Studio at Le Cannet.* (c.1942-43). Pencil and charcoal, 6¼ x 9¾". Private collection, Paris.

PRINTS

103. *France-Champagne,* poster. (1891). Color lithograph, 30½ x 22¾". Floury 1, R-M. 1. The Museum of Modern Art, New York. Purchase.

104. *Family Scene.* 1892. Color lithograph, 8⅝ x 10½". Floury 2, R-M. 2. The Museum of Modern Art, New York. Acquired through the Lillie P. Bliss Bequest. Ill. p. 17.

105. *Family Scene.* 1893. Color lithograph, 12⅜ x 7⅛". Floury 4, R-M. 4. The Museum of Modern Art, New York. Purchase.

Petites scènes familières, (1893). Illustrations for a music album by Claude Terrasse. Lithographs. Floury 5. The Museum of Modern Art, New York. Purchase.

106. *Au cirque. La Haute-Ecole.* 3⅛ x 9⅜". R-M. 23.

107. *Quadrille.* 4⅜ x 9¼". R-M. 24.

108. *Dogs.* (1893). Lithograph, 14⁷⁄₁₆ x 10¼", published in *L'Escarmouche*, December 10, 1893. Floury 6, R-M. 25. The Museum of Modern Art, New York. Gift of Abby Aldrich Rockefeller.

109. *Municipal Guard.* (1893). Lithograph, 10 x 6½", published in *L'Escarmouche*, December 31, 1893. Floury 7, R-M. 26. The Museum of Modern Art, New York. Gift of Abby Aldrich Rockefeller. Ill. p. 18.

110. *Young Girl with Black Stockings.* (1893). Lithograph, 11⁷⁄₁₆ x 5⁷⁄₁₆", published in *L'Escarmouche*, January 14, 1894. Floury 8, R-M. 27. The Museum of Modern Art, New York. Gift of Abby Aldrich Rockefeller. Ill. p. 21.

111. *Portrait.* (c. 1893). Lithograph, 11½ x 9¾", projected print for *L'Escarmouche*. Floury 9, R-M. 28. The Museum of Modern Art, New York. Gift of Abby Aldrich Rockefeller.

112. *La Revue Blanche*, poster. 1894. Color lithograph, 31½ x 21¼". Floury 10, R-M. 32. The Museum of Modern Art, New York. Purchase.

113. *Woman with Umbrella.* (1894). Color lithograph, 8⅝ x 5". Floury 12, R-M. 35. The Museum of Modern Art, New York. Abby Aldrich Rockefeller Fund.

114. *Nib.* (1895). Lithograph, 12¹⁵⁄₁₆ x 19¹¹⁄₁₆", supplement to *Revue Blanche*, April 1, 1895. R-M. 36. The Museum of Modern Art, New York. Purchase.

115. *Quelques aspects de la vie de Paris*, (1895), published by A. Vollard. Floury 16. Plate IV: *House in the Court.* Color lithograph, 13⅜ x 10¼". R-M. 59. The Museum of Modern Art, New York. Larry Aldrich Fund.

116. *Salon des Cent*, poster. 1896. Color lithograph, 22¾ x 15⅛". Floury 19, R-M. 45. The Museum of Modern Art, New York. Purchase.

117. *La Dernière Croisade.* (c. 1896). Program for the Théâtre de l'Oeuvre (proof printed before the text). Lithograph, 11⅞ x 19½". Floury 22, R-M. 39. The Museum of Modern Art, New York. Purchase. Ill. p. 2.

118. *L'Estampe et l'Affiche*, poster. (c. 1896). Color lithograph, 32 x 23½". Floury 23, R-M. 38. The Museum of Modern Art, New York. Purchase. Ill. p. 24.

119. *The Laundry Girl.* 1896. Color lithograph, 11⅝ x 7⅞". Floury 25, R-M. 42. The Museum of Modern Art, New York. Gift of Victor S. Riesenfeld. Ill. p. 20.

120. *Child with Lamp.* (1896). Color lithograph, 13⅛ x 18⅛". Floury 26, R-M. 43. The Museum of Modern Art, New York. Gift of Mrs. Bliss Parkinson. Ill. p. 13.

121. Cover for *L'Album d'estampes originales*, 1897. Color lithograph, 22¼ x 33½". Floury 24, R-M. 41. The Museum of Modern Art, New York, Purchase. Ill. p. 6.

122. *Boating.* (c. 1897). Color lithograph, 10⁹⁄₁₆ x 18½". Floury 27, R-M. 44. The Museum of Modern Art, New York. Gift of Abby Aldrich Rockefeller. Ill. p. 19.

123. *Malheureuse Adèle* from the *Répertoire du Théâtre des Pantins*, (1896-98). Cover for music sheet published by the *Mercure de France*. Text by Franc-Nohain, music by Terrasse. Lithograph, 12⅛ x 9⅛". Floury 32, R-M. 53. The Museum of Modern Art, New York. Purchase.

124. *Screen.* (1897). Color lithograph on four panels, each 53¼ x 17¾". Floury 35, R-M. 47. The Museum of Modern Art, New York. Abby Aldrich Rockefeller Fund.

125. *Horse Cabs.* (1897). Color lithograph for a screen, 7¹¹⁄₁₆ x 17¾". Floury 35, R-M. 47. The Museum of Modern Art, New York. Gift of Abby Aldrich Rockefeller.

126. *The Loge.* (1898). Frontispiece for Mellerio's *Lithographie originale en couleurs.* Color lithograph, 8¼ x 7⁷⁄₁₆". Floury 38, R-M. 73. The Museum of Modern Art, New York. Gift of Mrs. Edith G. Halpert. Ill. p. 12.

127. Illustration for *Parallèlement* by Paul Verlaine, published by Ambroise Vollard, Paris, (1900). Color lithograph, 9¾ x 8⅝". Floury 40, R-M. 94. The Museum of Modern Art, New York. Purchase.

128. *Salon d'Automne*, poster. (c. 1912). Color lithograph, 58 x 41⅞". The Museum of Modern Art, New York. Gift of Peter H. Deitsch.

129. *Portrait of Ambroise Vollard.* (c. 1914(?)). Etching, 13¹⁵⁄₁₆ x 9⅜". Floury 62. The Museum of Modern Art, New York. Purchase.

130. *Place Clichy.* (c. 1923). Color lithograph, 18¹⁵⁄₁₆ x 25³⁄₁₆". R-M. 77. Lent by The Art Institute of Chicago. Ill. p. 23.

131. Three illustrations for Mirbeau's *Dingo*, (1923). Soft ground etching and drypoint, 11¼ x 11⅞, 11¼ x 9, 12¹¹⁄₁₆ x 9¾". Floury 56. The Museum of Modern Art, New York. Gift of Mr. and Mrs. Walter Bareiss.

132. *Seated Woman.* (1925). Lithograph from portfolio *Pierre Bonnard, peintre et lithographe*, 13 x 8½". Floury 54, R-M. 83. The Museum of Modern Art, New York. Gift of Abby Aldrich Rockefeller. Ill. p. 115.

NOTE: Floury, see Terrasse, Bibliography, p. 111. R-M., see Roger-Marx, Bibliography, p. 111.

SELECTED BIBLIOGRAPHY
by Bernard Karpel, Librarian

Early in 1948 The Museum of Modern Art published for its Bonnard exhibition the first comprehensive monograph in English by John Rewald. It includes a bibliography of 225 citations (books, articles, catalogues and illustrated books) compiled by the undersigned. Since it is widely distributed and still in print, it seems unnecessary to repeat that inclusive body of references from 1893 to 1947. After recalling some of the major titles prior to 1947, the listing below begins with data from 1948 (No. 202) and carries it selectively until 1964 (No. 326). One should note the useful documentation in Terrasse (1927), updated by Natanson (bibl. 207), condensed in Vollmer (bibl. 255), and reviewed with varying degrees of thoroughness in other bibliographies cited here. The numbered references below are, with the temporary exception of three titles, in the Museum Library. Materials considered of secondary value on this occasion but accessible through *The Art Index* and *Répertoire d'Art et d'Archéologie* have not been reported. However, the references below, when joined to the Rewald data, constitute a total of 350 citations, adequate to the needs of both the lay and the scholarly researcher.

BASIC MONOGRAPHS: 1919-1947

WERTH, LÉON. Bonnard. Paris, Crées, 1919.
  Second edition, 1923.

COQUIOT, GUSTAVE. Bonnard. Paris, Bernheim-Jeune, 1922.

TERRASSE, CHARLES. Bonnard. Paris, Floury, 1927.
  Bibliography. List of illustrated works. Catalogue of graphic work by Jean Floury.

COURTHION, PIERRE. Bonnard: Peintre du merveilleux. Lausanne, Marguerat, 1945.

BEER, FRANÇOIS-JOACHIM. Pierre Bonnard. Marseille, Editions Françaises d'Art, 1947.
  Text also by Louis Gillet and Raymond Cogniat.

VERVE (Periodical). Couleur de Bonnard. Paris, Editions de la revue Verve, 1947.
  Published as v.5, no. 17-18, p.[1-84] incl. col. pl.

RECENT MONOGRAPHS & BOOKLETS: 1948-1964

202 REWALD, JOHN. Pierre Bonnard. New York, Museum of Modern Art, 1948. 152 p. ill. (col. pl.)
  Issued for exhibition (May 11-Sept. 6). Also "in collaboration with the Cleveland Museum of Art." Bibliography by B. Karpel, continued in bibl. 211.

203 REWALD, JOHN. Bonnard. New York, Published by Albert Carman for The Museum of Modern Art, 1948.
  Small folio of six color reproductions with brief introduction.

204 JEDLICKA, GOTTHARD. Pierre Bonnard. Ein Besuch. Erlenbach-Zürich, Rentsch, 1949. 247 p. ill.

205 SÖDERBERG, ROLF. Pierre Bonnard. Stockholm, Forum, 1949. 64 p. ill. (col. pl.).
  Brief bibliography.

206 ROGER-MARX, CLAUDE. Bonnard. Paris, Hazan, 1950. 14 p. col. pl. Bibliothèque Aldine, no. 18.

207 NATANSON, THADÉE. Tentatives: Le Bonnard que je propose, 1867-1947. Geneva, Cailler, 1951. 363 p. 266 ill. (pt. col.)
  "Documents," p. 231-244: chronology, illustrated books, catalogues, bibliography.

208 ROGER-MARX, CLAUDE. Bonnard lithographe. Monte Carlo, Editions du Livre-André Sauret, 1952. 184 p. incl. 98 pl. (pt. col.)
  Introduction by Claude Terrasse, p. 27-47. Descriptive text with plates.

209 RUMPEL, HEINRICH. Pierre Bonnard. Berne, Scherz, 1952. 32 p. 53 pl.
  Also translation published by Martello (Milan, 1952).

210 SUTTON, DENYS. Bonnard (1867-1947). London, Faber & Faber, 1957. 24 p. col. pl.
  Introduction and notes for mounted plates in the "Faber Gallery" series.

211 NEW YORK, MUSEUM OF MODERN ART. Bonnard and his Environment. Texts by James Thrall Soby, James Elliott and Monroe Wheeler. New York, Museum of Modern Art, distributed by Doubleday & Co., 1964. 116 p. ill. (col.pl.)
  Exhibition "in collaboration with the Art Institute of Chicago and the Los Angeles County Museum of Art." Catalogue of exhibits, chronology, bibliography, list of illustrated books.

GENERAL WORKS

212 ARLAND, MARCEL. Chronique de la peinture moderne. Paris, Corrêa, 1949. p. 83-85.

213 BARR, ALFRED H., JR. Masters of Modern Art. New York, Museum of Modern Art, 1954. p. 38-39, 215, 229, col. pl.

214 BENET, RAFAEL. Historia de la pintura moderna: Simbolismo. Barcelona, Omega, 1953. p. 361 (index) ill.

215 BERNHEIM-JEUNE, GALERIE. Catalogue raisonné de l'oeuvre complet de Pierre Bonnard. Paris, Editions J. & H. Bernheim-Jeune, [in preparation].
  Announced 1950 in bibl. 121.

216 CARCO, FRANCIS. L'Ami des peintres. Paris, Gallimard, 1953. p. 191-215.

217 CASSOU, JEAN [& OTHERS]. Gateway to the Twentieth Century. New York, McGraw-Hill, 1962. p. 22, 32, 60, 130-132, 343, ill. (col.).

218 COGNIAT, RAYMOND. Histoire de la peinture. v. 2, p. 238-239, 311 (index) Paris, Nathan, 1955.
  Complemented by his: French Painting of the Time of the Impressionists. New York, Paris, London: Hyperion, 1951. p. 150-151 ill.—The Century of the Impressionists. New York, Crown. 1960. p. 180, ill. Both include a general bibliography.

219 COURTHION, PIERRE. L'Art indépendant. Paris, Michel, 1958. p. 38-42, 302 (index) ill.

220 DORIVAL, BERNARD. Les étapes de la peinture française contemporaine. Paris, Gallimard, 1943-1946. 3 v., p. 340 (index, v. III).

221 DORIVAL, BERNARD, ed. Les Peintres célèbres. [Geneva & Paris], Mazenod, 1948.
   "Bonnard" by Georges Salles, p. 320-323. port., col. pl.

222 DORIVAL, BERNARD. Twentieth Century Painters: Nabis, Fauves, Cubists. New York, Universe, 1958. p. 19-31, 125 col. pl.
   Translated from the French (Paris, Tisné, 1957).

223 ÉTAPES DE L'ART FRANCAIS. Paris, Perrin, 1951. p. 151-154 ill.
   Includes Jean Rudel: Bonnard et la "matière" picturale. Originally published in Médecine de France no. 17, p. 29-32, ill. 1950.

224 FELS, FLORENT. L'Art vivant de 1900 à nos jours. Geneva, Cailler, 1950. p. 127-135 ill.

225 FRIEDENTHAL, RICHARD. Letters of the Great Artists. New York, Random House, 1963. p. 242-246 ill.

226 GAFFE, RENÉ. Introduction a la peinture française. Paris, Éditions des Artistes, 1954. p. 165-170 ill.

227 GARÇON, MAURICE. Le Procès de la succession Bonnard et le droit des artistes. Plaidoyer de Maurice Garçon, 10 novembre 1952. [Paris, 1952]. 104 p.
   Copy on deposit at the Frick Library and the Museum of Modern Art, New York.

228 HAFTMANN, WERNER. Painting of the Twentieth Century. New York, Praeger, 1960. v. 1, p. 419 (index); v. 2, p. 39 ill.
   Revised version of German edition (Munich, Prestel, 1954-57).

229 HERMANN, FRITZ. Die Revue blanche und die Nabis. Munich. Mikrocopie G. m. b. H., 1959. 2 v. ill.
   Extensive documentation. Bonnard references, v. 2, p. 435-436.

230 HERON, PATRICK. The Changing Forms of Art. London, Routledge & Kegan Paul, 1955. p. 116-129.
   "Pierre Bonnard and abstraction."

231 HESS, WALTER. Das Problem der Farbe in den Selbstzeugnissen moderner Maler. Munich, Prestel, 1953.
   General bibliography, p. 182-186. Also his: Die Farbe in der modernen Malerei. Munich, Universität München, 1950. Dissertation.

232 HUMBERT, AGNÈS. Les Nabis et leur époque. Geneva, Cailler, 1954. 152 p. ill.
   Bibliography.

233 JACCOTTET, PHILIP. French Drawing of the Twentieth Century. New York, Vanguard, 1955. p. 150-151, pl. 17-22.
   Also European edition.

234 LEYMARIE, JEAN. Impressionism. [Geneva?], Skira, 1955. p. 130 (index).
   General bibliography, p. 127-129.

235 LIBERMAN, ALEXANDER. The Artist in his Studio. New York, Viking, 1960. p. 18-20, pl. 16-20 (col.).

236 LHOTE, ANDRÉ. La Peinture libérée. Paris, Grasset, 1956. p. 203-213.

237 MATHEY, FRANÇOIS. The Impressionists. New York, Praeger, 1961. p. 201-203 ill. (col.).
   Translated from the French. Includes general chronology and bibliography.

238 MORNAND, PIERRE. Vingt-deux artistes du livre. Paris, Le Courrier graphique, 1948. p. 39-48, 292-293 ill.
   Bibliography. Preface by J.-R. Thomé.

239 NACENTA, RAYMOND. School of Paris. Greenwich, Conn., New York Graphic Society, 1960. p. 285 col. pl.
   "The painters and the artistic climate of Paris since 1900."

240 NATANSON, THADÉE. Peints à leur tour. Paris, Michel, 1948. p. 316-342.
   Complemented in his: Un Henri de Toulouse-Lautrec. 1951. p. 168-172.

241 NEWTON, ERIC. In My View. London, etc., Longmans, Green [1950].
   Reviews "Bonnard and his Contemporaries," Lefèvre Gallery, London, June 1947.

242 NOVOTNY, FRITZ. Die grossen französischen Impressionisten. Vienna, Schroll, 1952. p. 61-62, pl. 40.

243 PANORAMA DE L'ART PRESÉNT. Paris, Éditions Prisme des Arts, 1957.
   Includes Raymond Cogniat: "Bonnard, le révolutionnaire."

244 PANORAMA DES ARTS. Paris, Somogny, 1948. p. 24-26, 206-210 ill.
   R. C.: "La mort de Bonnard."—J. L.: "Rétrospective Bonnard."

245 RAUCH, NICOLAS. Les peintres et les livres. Geneva, N. Rauch, 1957. p. 29-39 ill.

246 RAYNAL, MAURICE. [& OTHERS]. History of Modern Painting: From Baudelaire to Bonnard. Geneva, Skira, 1949. p. 101-112, 115-116. col. pl.
   Chronology and bibliography. Also European editions.

247 RAYNAL, MAURICE. Modern Painting. Geneva, Skira, 1953. p. 327 (index).
   Chronology, bibliography (p. 294-295). Also general bibliography. Also European and revised editions.

248 REWALD, JOHN. Post-Impressionism from Van Gogh to Gauguin. 2.ed. New York, Museum of Modern Art, 1957. p. 604 (index) ill.

249 ROGER-MARX, CLAUDE. Graphic Art—the 19th Century. New York, etc., McGraw-Hill, 1962. p. 249 (index) ill.
   Translated from the French (Éditions Somogny).

250 SERT, MISIA. Misia and the Muses. New York, Day, 1953. p. 215 (index).

251 STERLING, CHARLES. Still Life Painting. New York, Universe, 1957. p. 159, pl. 105.
   "From Monet to Bonnard," p. 99 ff. Translated from the revised edition (Paris, Tisné, 1959).

252 STUBBE, WOLF. Die Graphik des zwannzigsten Jahrhunderts. Berlin, Rembrandt, 1962. p. 27-28, 256; pl. 47.

253 VERLAINE, PAUL. Parallèlement. Monte-Carlo, Éditions du Cap, 1957.
   Reduced facsimile with Bonnard illustrations for the Vollard edition, 1900.

254 VOLLARD, AMBROISE. Erinnerungen eines Kunsthändlers. Zurich, Diogenes, 1957. p. 366 ill.
   With bibliography of the Vollard editions.

255 VOLLMER, HANS. Allgemeines Lexikon der bildenden Künstler des XX. Jahrhunderts. Leipzig, Seemann, 1953. v. 1. p. 263.
   Bibliographical notes.

256 WINTERTHUR. KUNSTMUSEUM. Hauptwerke des Kunstmuseum Winterthur. Winterthur, 1949. p. 146-156 ill.
   Includes Hedy Hahnloser-Bühler on two Bonnard paintings.

ARTICLES

257 ALFORD, JOHN. Bonnard's art for art's sake . . . *Art News* 47:16-20, 60 ill. June 1948.
   On exhibition at The Museum of Modern Art.

258 BEER, FRANÇOIS-JOACHIM. Le souvenir de Pierre Bonnard. *Prisme des Arts* no. 13: V 1957.

259 BETTEMS, ANNE. Bonnard. *Pour l'Art* no. 13:23-24 ill. 1950.

260 BONNARD: LAST OF THE GREAT FRENCH IMPRESSIONISTS . . . *Life* v. 25 no. 3: 52-56 ill. (col.) July 19, 1948.
   Show at the Museum of Modern Art.

261 CATLIN, STANTON L. Pierre Bonnard's "Dining Room in the Country." *Bulletin of the Minneapolis Institute of Arts* v. 44 no. 6: 41-51 ill. (col.) Nov. 1955.

262 CASSOU, JEAN. Dessins des peintres et sculpteurs de l'école de Paris. *Art et Style* no. 48-49 ill. 1958.
   Special number (4p., 64 pl.).

263 CHETHAM, CHARLES S. "Still life by Evening Light, 1927" by Pierre Bonnard. *Fogg Art Museum Annual* p. 49-51 ill. 1956-57.
   Additional text in: Drawings & Sculpture collected by Louise and Joseph Pulitzer, Jr. New York, Knoedler; Cambridge, Gogg Art Museum, 1957. p. 15-19 ill.

264 COMPARD, ÉMILE. Souvenirs sur P. Bonnard et F. Fénéon. *Ring des Arts* no 3:22-23 Noël 1962.
   English translation, p. V-VI.

265 COMSTOCK, HELEN. Bonnard memorial exhibitions at Cleveland and Museum of Modern Art. *Connoisseur* 122:38 Sept. 1948.
   Similarly *Art News* 47:30 Mar. 1948, *Art Digest* 22:10 May 15, 1948, 22:32-33 June 1948, 22:21 Aug. 1948, *Arts* (Paris) p.3 Mar. 19, 1948.

266 COUTURIER, M. A. L'Église d'Assy en Haute-Savoie. *Art et Décoration* no. 16:19 ff ill. 1950.
   Associated artists include Bonnard.

267 DARDENNE, ROGER. On a vendu les oeuvres qui composaient la collection du peintre Pierre Bonnard. *France Illustration* no. 408:82-83 Mar. 1954.
   Also previous article: Un faux testament . . . l'affaire Bonnard. no. 368:474-476 ill. Nov. 1952.

268 DEVÉMY, J. Visites à Bonnard. *L'Art Sacré* no. 1-2:8-9 ill. Sept.-Oct. 1950.
   Also texts by M. A. Couturier.

269 DU COLOMBIER, PIERRE. Qu'est-ce que le Nabis? *Jardin des Arts* no. 8:501-509 ill. 1955.

270 FRANCIS, HENRY S. The art of Pierre Bonnard. *Bulletin of the Cleveland Museum of Art* 37:5-8 ill. Jan. 1950.

271 GAUTHIER, E. PAUL. Lithographs of the Revue blanche. *Magazine of Art* v. 45:273-278 ill. Oct. 1952.

272 GEIST, SIDNEY. Devotee of color. *Art Digest* 28:9 ill. Jan. 15, 1954.
   On exhibition at the Fine Arts Associates. Also reviewed in *Art News* 52:29 ill. Feb. 1954, *Arts & Architecture* 71: 6-7 Mar. 1954.

273 GIRARD, ANDRÉ. Pierre Bonnard. *Vogue* p. 108-111, 151-152 ill. (col.) June 1948.
   GRADMANN, ERWIN. Bonnard-Vuillard. 1952. See bibl.325

274 GROSCHWITZ, GUSTAVE VON. The significance of XIX century lithography. *Gazette des Beaux-Arts* v. 44:243-266 ill. 1954.
   On color lithography as an independent art. Reproductions include Bonnard.

275 GUÉGUEN, PIERRE. Bonnard l'enchanteur. *XXe Siècle* no. 13:13-17 ill. (col.) Noël 1959.
   English summary, p. 111, 113. Originally published in first series, no. 2, 1938.

276 HOFER, PHILIP. Some precursors of the modern illustrated book. *Harvard Library Bulletin* 4:191-202 ill. 1950.
   Complemented by: Four modern illustrated bestiaries. *Gazette des Beaux-Arts*. 33:301-316 ill. 1948. On Lautrec, Bonnard, Dufy and Picasso.

277 HUMBERT, AGNES. Ceux qui vont devenir des Nabis. *Art-Documents* no. 6:8-9 ill. 1951.

278 JOËTS, JULES. Deux grands peintres au Cannet . . . Le dernier entretien de Pierre Bonnard. *Art-Documents* no.29:8-9 ill. 1953.

279 JOHNSON, LINCOLN F. Pierre Bonnard and impressionism. *Baltimore Museum Art News* 17:1-16 ill. Dec. 1953.

280 JONNSON, UNA. E. Lithographs of Pierre Bonnard. *Brooklyn Museum Bulletin* 11 no. 2:1-9 ill. 1950.
   "With list of prints in the Museum."

281 LIBERMAN, ALEXANDER. Bonnard. *Vogue* 128:156-159 ill. Oct. 1, 1956.
   Similar coverage in bibl.40.

282 LUFT, PETER. Bonnard et Vuillard en Allemagne. *Prisme des Arts* no. 12:1-4 ill. 1957.

283 MARTINI, ALBERTO. Gli inizi difficili di Pierre Bonnard. *Arte Antica e Moderna* 1:255-279 ill. 1958.

284 MINNEAPOLIS: POST-IMPRESSIONIST BONNARD. *Art News* 55: 30-31 ill. May 1956.
   Similar coverage: *Arts* (New York) 30:8 Feb. 1956.

285 MORAND, KATHLEEN. "Bonnard et son époque" [exhibition in Paris]. *Burlington Magazine* 102:275 ill. June 1960.
   Also "Bonnard paintings at Galerie Bellier," 103:36 Jan. 1961.

286 MULLALY, TERENCE. French painting and the Japanese print. *Apollo* 62:192-196 ill. 1955.

287 PAYNE, E. H. "Interior" by Pierre Bonnard. *Detroit Institute Bulletin* 40 no. 1:10-11 ill. 1960-61.

288 PHILLIPS, DUNCAN. Pierre Bonnard. *Kenyon Review* 2 no. 4: 561-566 ill. (col.) Autumn 1949.
Reprinted in bibl.127.

289 NATANSON, THADÉE. Le Bonnard que je propose. *Art-Documents* no. 1:7 ill. Oct. 1950.
Extract from bibl.12.

290 PERRUCHOT, HENRI. L'affaire Bonnard. *L'Oeil* no. 21:10-15 ill. Oct. 1958.
Similar coverage: L'affaire Bonnard. *Connaissance des Arts* no. 9:18-19 ill. 1952.—Le procès Bonnard. *Arts* no. 311: 1, 4 May 18, 1951.

291 OMAGGIO A BONNARD. *Emporium* 107 no. 638:50-57 ill. Feb. 1948.
Critiques on the Orangerie retrospective.

292 PIA, PASCAL. Ambroise Vollard, marchand et éditeur. *L'Oeil* no. 3:18-27 ill. 1955.

293 ROH, FRANZ. Bonnards Wunder der Farbe. *Kunst* 51:161-164 ill. 1952-53.

294 RUHEMANN, HELMUT. Methods of the masters, III: Five modern masters. *Studio* 145:72-77 ill. 1953.

295 SALOMON, JACQUES. Mon ami Bonnard. *Arts* no. 797:8 ill. Nov. 23-29, 1960.

296 SELVIG, FORREST. Les Nabis: prophets of the vanguard. *Art News* 61:34-37, 64-66 Dec. 1962.
On exhibit at the Minneapolis Institute.

297 SOBY, JAMES T. Last of the Impressionists: Pierre Bonnard. *Town & Country* 102:70-71, 90, 92, 94 ill. (col.).

298 STRALEM, JEAN & DONALD. The Nabis and their circle. *Minneapolis Institute Bulletin* 51:129-134 Dec. 1962.
Includes chronology, catalogue of exhibition, bibliography. Also note bibl. 95, 102.

299 SUTTON, DENYS. The "Revue Blanche." *Signature* (n.s.) no. 18:21-43 ill. 1954.
Includes brief French text by Natanson on Bonnard (Jan. 15, 1896). Also see Sutton's "Bonnard and his French contemporaries," *Burlington Magazine* June 1947.

300 TERRASSE, CLAUDE. Bonnard. *Art News Annual* 28:84-107, 32 ill. (12 col.) 1959.

301 THOMÉ, J. R. Pierre Bonnard (1867-1947), graveur et illustrateur. *Courrier Graphique* 24 no. 105:3-10 ill. Sept.-Oct. 1959.

302 TOWNDRON, KENNETH R. French painters, II: Bonnard. *Apollo* 55:79-83 ill. 1952.
On current London show.

303 WALDVOGEL, MELVIN. The Nabis and their circle, 1890-1900. *Art International* 7 no. 1:55-58 Jan. 25, 1963.
On exhibit at Minneapolis, Nov. 15-Dec. 30.

304 WALDVOGEL, MELVIN. Bonnard and Vuillard as lithographers. *Minneapolis Institute Bulletin* 52:66-81 Sept. 1963.
Bibliography.

305 WERTH, LÉON. Pierre Bonnard, illustrateur. *Portique* no. 7:9-20 ill. 1950.
"Essai de bibliographie des ouvrages illustrés par Pierre Bonnard," p. 19-20.

306 [ZERVOS, CHRISTIAN]. Liste des principales oeuvres françaises au Musée d'Art Moderne Occidental à Moscou. *Cahiers d'Art* 25 no.2:337 1950.
No. 1-14:Bonnard.

EXHIBITION CATALOGUES

307 BASEL. KUNSTHALLE. Pierre Bonnard. May 28-July 17, 1955. [60]p. 28 ill.
173 exhibits. Texts by R. T. Stoll and Charles Terrasse. Chronology, bibliography. Reviewed *Werk* 42:166 (suppl.) Aug. 1956.

308 BERNE, KUNSTHALLE. Der Maler der Revue Blanche. Mar. 21-Apr. 22, 1951.
No. 1-76 by Bonnard. Texts by Fritz Hermann, Arnold Rüdlinger. Chronology. Bibliography by Hans Bolliger. Complemented by: Estampes des Peintres de la "Revue blanche." Berne, Gutekunst & Klipstein, 1952. (Sales catalogue no. 50).

309 BOSTON. MUSEUM OF FINE ARTS. The Artist and the Book in Western Europe and the United States, 1860-1960. Boston, The Museum; Cambridge, Harvard College, 1961. Exhibited at Boston, May 4-July 16. Bonnard, p. 24-27 (ill.). Introduction by Philip Hofer; research and compilation by Eleanor M. Garvey and others. General bibliography.

310 BRUNSWICK. KUNSTVEREIN. Pierre Bonnard. Braunschweig, Nov. 11-Dec. 16, 1956. 40 p. incl. 28 pl. (col.).
Bibliography. Exhibit also shown at Bremen, Cologne.

311 BRUSSELS. PALAIS DES BEAUX ARTS. Le Mouvement symboliste. Jan. 31, 1956—Mar. 3, 1957.
Published by Éditions de la Connaissance. Bonnard, p. 133 (index). Exhibit on the cultural situation, including works of art, documents, editions. Prefaces by G. Bauer, R. Guiette.

312 EDINBURGH. ROYAL SCOTTISH ACADEMY. Exhibition of Paintings by Pierre Bonnard & Edouard Vuillard. Aug. 17-Sept. 18, 1948.
Published by the Arts Council of Great Britain. 55 exhibits by Bonnard (9 ill.), also 11 lithographs. "Last of the impressionists, called in the nineties *Symbolistes, Synthétistes, Intimistes, Classicistes, Idéistes* . . ."

313 LONDON. MARLBOROUGH LTD. Roussel, Bonnard, Vuillard. May 5-June 12, 1954.
No. 34-59 by Bonnard (8 ill.). Preface by John Russell. Varied texts including G. Geffroy on Bonnard (1896), also Signac, Denis, Gide. Chronology, bibliography. For review of later Bonnard exhibition see M. Amaya in *Apollo* 77:49 ill. Jan. 1963.

314 LYON. MUSÉE. Bonnard. Festival de Lyon-Charbonniers, 1954. 53p. incl. 17 ill.
Catalogue of 106 exhibits by M. Rocher-Jauneau with critical notes. Text by Charles Terrasse, René Jullian. Chronology, bibliography.

315 MILAN. ENTE MANIFESTAZIONI MILANESI. Pierre Bonnard. Apr.-May 1955. 78p. 66pl. (col.).
Catalogue of 103 exhibits and essay by Franco Russoli. Foreword by L. Morandi. Essay by Charles Terrasse (also in French). Bibliography, p.74-78. Shown also in Basel and Nice. Edition published by Silvana (Milano). Reviewed in *Arte Lombardo* 2:203-205 1956, *Arti* no. 1:I-IV, 6-22 1955, *Biennale di Venezia* no. 204:42-43 1955, *Domus*, no.309:48-49 1955, *Emporium* 121:265-272 1955.

316 NICE. MUSÉE DES PONCHETTES. Bonnard. Aug.-Sept. 1955.
44p. ill.
Lists 78 exhibits. Preface by Charles Terrasse. Edited by
Madeleine Guynet-Pechadre. Bibliography. Reviewed
Arts (Paris) no. 532:8 Sept. 7-13, 1955.

317 PARIS. BERNHEIM-JEUNE & CIE. Exposition rétrospective:
Bonnard. May-July 1950. 24p. ill.
62 exhibits. Preface by Charles Terrasse. For later "Hom-
mage à Bonnard" see *Studio* 152:91 Sept. 1956.

318 PARIS. MAISON DE LA PENSÉE FRANÇAISE. Bonnard. June
1955. 18 ill.
Introduction by Georges Besson. Reviewed in *Arts (Paris)*
no. 522:511 ill. June 29-July 5, 1955, *Art News* 54:47
Sept. 1955.

319 PARIS. MUSÉE NATIONAL D'ART MODERNE. Bonnard,
Vuillard et les Nabis, 1888-1903. June 8-Oct. 2, 1955.
109p. 24 ill.
Catalogue by Bernard Dorival and Agnès Humbert published by Éditions des Musées Nationaux (1955). Reviewed
in *Arts (Paris)* no.520:14-21 June 1955, *Burlington Magazine* 97:267 Aug. 1955, *Emporium* 122:218-224 1955.

320 PARIS. MUSÉE DE L'ORANGERIE. Exposition Bonnard. Catalogue. 2.éd. Paris, Éditions des Musées Nationaux, 1948.
24p. ill.
First edition for show held Oct.-Nov. 1947.

321 ROTTERDAM. MUSEUM BOYMANS. Bonnard. 1953.
16p. 36 ill.
129 exhibits. Introduction by Charles Terrasse in Dutch
and French. Chronology.

322 VENICE. ESPOSIZIONE BIENNALE INTERNAZIONALE D'ARTE.
XXV. Catalogo. 1950.
Bonnard section, with essay by Raymond Cogniat, p.285-
286. Critique by Bernard Dorival in *Biennale di Venezia*
no. 1:18-22 1950.

323 WASHINGTON. PHILLIPS GALLERY. Six Paintings by Bon-
nard. Jan. 12-Feb. 12, 1958. 12 ill.
"A loan exhibition" with text by Duncan Phillips. Titled
"A bulletin," the essay is reprinted from bibl.92.

324 WILLIAMSTOWN (Mass.). STERLING AND FRANCINE CLARK
INSTITUTE. Exhibition 24: Pierre Bonnard Lithographs.
Aug. 1963.
19 exhibits (18pl.). Reviewed *American Artist* 27:8 Oct.
1963.

325 ZURICH. EIDGENOSSISCHE TECHNISCHE HOCHSCHULE. Bonnard-Vuillard: Handzeichnungen, Druckgraphik. Feb. 23-
Apr. 27, 1952. 17p. cover ill.
No catalogue listing, only "Einfuhrung von Erwin Gradmann." Reviewed in *Kunst und Volk* 14:39 1952, *Werk*
39 no. 4:48 (suppl.) Apr. 1952.

326 ZURICH. KUNSTHAUS. Pierre Bonnard, 1867-1947. June 6-
July 24 1949. 38p. ill.
247 exhibits. Texts by J. Leymarie and W. Wartmann in
French and German. Reviewed in *Kunst und Volk* 11 no. 3:
72-74 1949, *Werk* 36:107 (suppl.) Aug. 1949.

Seated Woman. (1925). Lithograph from portfolio *Pierre Bonnard,
peintre et lithographe,* 13 x 8½". The Museum of Modern Art,
New York. Gift of Abby Aldrich Rockefeller

WORKS ILLUSTRATED BY BONNARD

Asterisk indicates book in the Louis E. Stern Collection of Illustrated Books at The Museum of Modern Art.

JOZE, VICTOR, Reine de joie, moeurs du demi-monde. Paris, H. Julien, 1892. Lithograph (cover).

TERRASSE, CLAUDE. Petites scènes familières pour piano. Paris, Fromont, 1893. 19 lithographs and cover.

* TERRASSE, CLAUDE. Petit solfège illustré. Paris, Ancienne Maison Quantin, 1893. 30 lithographs and covers.

MELLERIO, ANDRÉ. La Lithographie originale en couleurs. Paris, L'Estampe et l'Affiche, 1898. 2 lithographs (cover and frontispiece).

* NANSEN, PETER, Marie. Paris, La Revue Blanche, 1898. 19 ink drawings (line cuts).

JARRY, ALFRED. Almanach du Père Ubu illustré. Paris, 1899. Ink drawings.

* COURTELINE, GEORGES and TERRASSE, CLAUDE. Pantheon-Courcelles. Paris, P. Dupont, (1900). Lithograph (cover and frontispiece).

* VERLAINE, PAUL. Parallèlement. Paris, Ambroise Vollard, 1900. 109 lithographs and 9 wood engravings.

* JARRY, ALFRED. Almanach illustré du Père Ubu pour le XXe siècle. Paris, 1901. 47 ink drawings (lithographs).

* LONGUS. Les Pastorales, ou Daphnis et Chloé. Paris, Ambroise Vollard, 1902. 151 lithographs.

BOYLESVE, RENÉ. La leçon d'amour dans un parc. Paris, La Revue Blanche, 1902. Cover.

RENARD, JULES. Histoires naturelles. Paris, Ernest Flammarion (1904). 67 ink drawings (line cuts).

* MIRBEAU, OCTAVE. La 628-E8. Paris, Charpentier et Fasquelle, 1908. 104 ink drawings (line cuts).

EBERHARDT, ISABELLE. Notes de route. Maroc—Algérie—Tunisie. 1908. 1 drawing by Bonnard (line cut).

BARRUCAND, VICTOR. D'un pays plus beau. Paris, Floury, 1910. 7 drawings.

GEFFROY, GUSTAVE. Preface to Germinal, album of prints. Paris, La Maison moderne, (c. 1910). 1 print by Bonnard.

MIRBEAU, OCTAVE and others. Cézanne. Paris, Bernheim Jeune, 1914. 1 lithograph by Bonnard after a Cézanne painting.

Catalogue of the *Salon d'Automne*. Paris. 1912. Cover.

* VOLLARD, AMBROISE. Le Père Ubu à l'hôpital. Paris, 1916. 2 ink drawings (line cuts).

* VOLLARD, AMBROISE. Le Père Ubu à l'aviation. Paris, Editions Georges Crés. 1918. 2 ink drawings (line cuts).

* GIDE, ANDRÉ. Der schlecht gefesselte Prometheus. Berlin, Hyperionverlag, 1919. 6 ink drawings (halftone).

* GIDE, ANDRÉ. Le Prométhée mal enchaîné. Paris, Nouvelle Revue Française, 1920. 30 drawings (line cuts).

ANET, CLAUDE. Notes sur l'amour. Paris, Crès, 1922. 14 drawings (engraved on wood by Yvonne Malliez).

* CHAUVEAU, LEOPOLD. Histoire du poisson scie et du poisson marteau. Paris, Payot, 1923. 38 drawings (line cuts).

GOMEZ DE LA SERNA, R. Seins. Paris, Crès, Les Cahiers d'Aujourd'hui, 1924. Drawings.

* MIRBEAU, OCTAVE. Dingo. Paris, Ambroise Vollard, 1924. 55 etchings.

FRAPIER, ed. Maîtres et petits maîtres d'aujourd'hui: Pierre Bonnard peintre et lithographe, text by C. Roger-Marx. Paris, Frapier, 1925. 4 lithographs.

* COQUIOT, GUSTAVE. En suivant la Seine. Paris, Delpeuch, 1926. 3 drawings.

* CHAUVEAU, LEOPOLD. Histoire du Petit Renaud. Paris, Nouvelle Revue Française, 1927. 49 drawings (pochoir).

TERRASSE, CLAUDE. Bonnard. Paris, Floury, 1927. 1 drypoint.

* Tableaux de Paris. Paris, Emile-Paul, 1927. 1 lithograph by Bonnard.

* ROGER-MARX, CLAUDE. Simili. Paris, Au Sans Pareil, 1930. 7 drypoints.

* VOLLARD, AMBROISE. La vie de Sainte Monique. Paris, Ambroise Vollard, 1930. 17 etchings, 29 drawings (transfer lithographs) and 178 woodcuts designed by Bonnard.

Paris 1937. Paris, Daragnes, 1937. 1 etching for BEDEL, MAURICE. "Faubourg Saint-Honoré."

* BONNARD, PIERRE. Correspondances. Paris, "Verve," ed. Tériade, 1944. 28 drawings (halftone).

* LOUYS, PIERRE. Le crepuscule des nymphes. Paris, Pierre Tisné, 1946. 24 lithographs.

COLETTE. Belles saisons. Paris, Club des lecteurs de la "Gazette des Lettres," 1947. Drawings.

VERVE. Couleur de Bonnard. Paris, "Verve," ed. Tériade, 1947. Cover, frontispiece, and all decorations designed by Bonnard.

FRONT COVER: *Dining Room in the Country, Vernon.* 1913. Oil, 64½ x 80". The Minneapolis Institute of Art

DATE DUE

PRINTED IN U.S.A.